Christmas Dolls

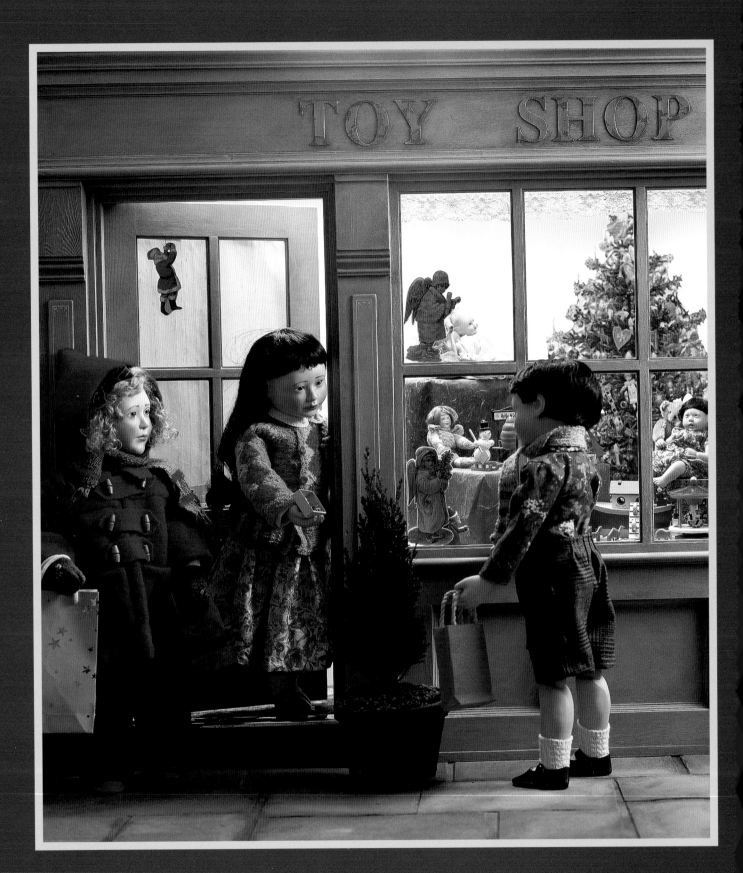

Christmas Dolls

JOAN MUYSKENS PURSLEY

Reverie

PUBLISHING COMPANY

DEDICATION

I dedicate this book to my mother, Jean Muyskens, and my late father, the
Reverend Cornelius P. Muyskens, who (with my sister, Jeanne, and three brothers,
Dirk, Don and Douw) made my memories of childhood so very special, and
filled all of my early Christmases with love and joy.

First edition/First printing

To purchase additional copies of this book, please contact:
Reverie Publishing Company
130 South Wineow Street, Cumberland, MD 21502
888-721-4999
www.reveriepublishing.com

Library of Congress Control Number 2005928735
ISBN 1-932485-25-2

Design: Jaye Medalia
Project Editor: Krystyna Poray Goddu

Front cover: Wenceslas Santa by Jan Coe

Back cover, clockwise from left: North Pole Riley by Helen Kish; Sophie by Angela and John Barker; Ann Estelle by
Mary Englebreit, "Queen of Christmas" by the Tonner Doll Company; Advent Angel by Elizabeth Jenkins

Page 2: Violet, Henrietta and Sam, each 21 inches, porcelain heads, wooden bodies and limbs,
limited to editions of 75 each, by Lynne and Michael Roche

Printed and bound in Korea

Contents

Introduction

Love came down at Christmas, Love all lovely, Love divine;
Love was born at Christmas, Stars and angels gave the sign.

HE STORIES, SMELLS, TASTES AND SONGS OF CHRISTMAS
make it a favorite holiday of literally millions of people around the world. The symbols of Christmas
are many, but first and foremost are those based on the Biblical story of Christ's birth: the crèche, angels
and the star.

For Christians, one of the most poignant stories in the Bible is the birth of Jesus. Told in the
Gospels, it is a story of faith and hope, full of incredible women and men and wondrous beings. There
are the elderly Elizabeth and Zechariah, parents of John the Baptist. There's Elizabeth's young cousin,
Mary, the mother of Jesus. There's Joseph, who, after being visited by an angel, agrees to take the preg-
nant Mary for his wife. There are shepherds, who see heavenly hosts singing of peace and good will to
men, and exotic wise men from Persia who follow a star to Bethlehem and find Mary and Joseph and
Baby Jesus sheltered in a stable because they could not get a room in an inn.

What hardships young Mary and Joseph must have experienced in making the trip to Bethlehem
while she was in her eighth month of pregnancy, and finally arriving to find no available accommoda-
tions in the town. One wonders how many places Joseph visited before finding a kind innkeeper who
allowed them to take shelter in his stable. The young couple was no doubt relieved to get off the streets
and have a modicum of privacy, but then Mary went into labor. Perhaps they had help with the birth,
perhaps not. The Bible doesn't tell us. But we do know that the mother and baby survived. Were
stable hands in and out during this difficult time? And what did the innkeeper and guests in the inn think
about the shepherds coming into Bethlehem to look at the newborn babe, and later strange magi appear-
ing with expensive gifts? The written record of Christ's birth leaves much to be imagined, which is one
of the reasons it is so personal, so heartening, to so many people around the world.

Centuries of artists have been inspired by this story, including some of today's dollmakers. Their
interpretations of Mary, Joseph and the Baby Jesus, along with those who visited the newborn babe, are
featured in the opening chapter of this book. Chapter two is filled with angel dolls.

The spirit of Christmas has inspired many secular stories, songs, poems and even a magical
ballet. Dolls depicting the characters from some of these also appear in this book. There are, for example, many magnificent Santa dolls, some based on the Bishop of Myra, considered by many to be the
inspiration for the modern Santa Claus, some reflecting European legends of Christmas gift givers, and

some depicting the Saint Nicholas of Clement C. Moore's famous poem, "The Night Before Christmas." Then there are modern-day Santas that come solely from the creative minds of the artists who made them. Also found within this book are dolls based on the characters of Charles Dickens' famous *A Christmas Carol*, and on the magical *The Nutcracker* ballet.

Not overlooked are more traditional Christmas dolls: babies and children dressed for the festive season, and fabulous fashion dolls all decked out for the holidays. Carolers, too, appear in these pages, reminding us not only of the wonderful songs of Christmas, but also of the tradition of bringing cheer to others through singing in the streets, in hospitals and nursing homes, and all around the town.

Another way of spreading the joy of Christmas is through decorating homes and yards. Christmas dolls can add wonderful holiday touches to your décor. Small dolls, for example, can be used to decorate a tree or a wreath. Larger ones make dramatic focal points for table centerpieces and mantle displays. You can tuck dolls amid the packages under your Christmas tree, have one or two popping out of stockings hung by the mantel with care, and dress a few to create a nativity scene. (Don't hesitate to use child dolls to depict the Holy Family—after all, children's pageants of the Christmas story have been held in churches and Sunday schools around the world for years.) Bring out the antique dolls in your collection to remind you and guests of Christmases past. In addition, if you have antique carriages, cribs or old rocking chairs, fill them with dolls—old or new—and make them an integral part of your holiday décor.

After December 25th, when the under-the-tree presents have been opened, pop your festive Christmas children into all those empty gift boxes littered about. First, line the boxes with acid-free tissue, and then add a bow or three to the front of each; you'll have such a charming display that you'll never want to put your tree away.

A few words of caution, though. Don't light candles near your dolls, and keep live greenery away from their delicate outfits. It's also wise to keep your dolls out of bright sunlight; it fades their clothing and may have an adverse effect on the faces and bodies of some antiques. Other than following those few simple rules, you can use your imagination and talent to deck your halls with dolls.

Pepper Hume, Mary and Joseph with the Child, 13 inches; Mary and Joseph: Super Sculpey heads and hands, cloth bodies and limbs with wire armatures; Baby: all Super Sculpey, one-of-a-kind

CHAPTER ONE

Nativity Figures

Away in a manger, no crib for a bed,
The little Lord Jesus lay down His sweet head.

Peter Wolf, Black-A-Moor (one of the three
Wise Men), 16 inches, Fimo head and limbs,
cloth and wire body, from one-of-a-kind set

HEN DOLL ARTIST MARILYN BOLDEN THINKS OF FAMILY
Christmases past, the first thing that comes to mind is the annual ritual of setting up their nativity scene. "As a child," she recalls, "I was
allowed to arrange the figures every year. At first, we had only the
Holy Family and the stable. Each year we would add a new piece to
the set. I have very special memories of going shopping to pick out
the new figure. I still have this family nativity set, and it is very
special to me. The cow has lost its horns, and several of the sheep
have only three legs, but I wouldn't part with it for anything."

Crèches are also part of Dutch artist Ankie Daanen's holiday
celebration. A few years ago, when she celebrated Christmas in
Spain, she and her grandchildren, all of whom were then four and
five years old, worked together to make a Christmas cradle with a little Jesus, plus Mother Mary and Joseph. "The next day was a sunny
day, and in the morning," the artist says, "the youngest of the grandchildren came to our bedroom and asked, 'May I take little Jesus and
Joseph today with me to the beach?'"

For Christians around the world, the setting up of a nativity
scene marks the beginning of the Christmas season. Memories of
that activity, such as those shared here by Bolden and Daanen, are
repeated year after year, as family members work together to set up
the stable and arrange the various figures. These and other reminis-
cences of Christmastimes gone by become part of a family's verbal
history.

The ritual of replicating the setting of Christ's birth has its roots
in 1223, when St. Francis of Assisi staged the first re-creation of it
by arranging real people and animals in a stable on Christmas Eve.
Some 350 years later, in 1562, the Jesuit church in Prague created a

Wendy Lawton, Lawton Doll Company, The Little Drummer Boy, 14 inches, all porcelain, limited to an edition of 500

COSTUMES, PROPS & SETTINGS

"Christmas dolls evoke so many happy memories for me," says Nancy DiPonte. "Among my favorites is when, as a sixth grader at St. Patrick School, I was chosen to depict Mary in the school's annual Christmas production. My mother and grandmother lovingly sewed my costume: a long white gown with a blue ribbon sash and a blue veil. The Baby Jesus I carried was my mom's own baby doll, which she had given to me a few years earlier. Although I remembered all my lines and I didn't drop my baby doll (what worries children have), I have no regrets that this was my first and only foray into the world of live theater."

Another of the artist's favorite memories is of the annual visit her family made to a house in their neighborhood, where an almost life-sized nativity tableau filled the front lawn. "It was complete with a large stable, brightly lit stars in the trees and softly playing Christmas carols. I would beg to visit it every year, and I will never forget the feeling of the cold winter air, the stillness of the dark night and the sense of peace that radiated from that scene.

"These memories influence my nativity dolls," DiPonte says. "I want to convey the tender love of Mary as she cradled her newly born Son, the gentle watchfulness of Joseph, and the peace, hope and love of God, which is the foundation of every Christmas celebration."

nativity scene inside its building. Other churches followed suit, and eventually the custom of creating a Christmas crèche inside not only churches, but also homes, had spread to all corners of the earth.

South Carolina cloth dollmaker Sandi Tucker has fond memories of her family's nativity scene, which decorated their front yard, along with a plethora of other holiday items. During her grade-school years, her family lived in Denver, which at that time held citywide competitions for best house decorations. "My folks participated every year, always expanding on the year before," says Tucker. "We had a full-size plywood cutout and painted nativity in the center of the yard, highlighted with spotlights. On either side of the nativity were crossed candy canes my parents made from stove piping and wide red-plastic ribbons. We had Santa and his nine reindeer on the roof—of course, there had to be nine once Rudolph entered the picture; they were highlighted with red and green spots. The patio was strung with multi-

TOP: Ankie Daanen, Three Kings Bring Presents, 15 inches, porcelain heads, arms and legs, stoneclay bodies, one-of-a-kinds

LEFT: Ankie Daanen, A Newborn King, 15 inches, porcelain head, arms and legs, stoneclay body, one-of-a-kind

Rotraut Schrott, Fatschenkind (a Bavarian version of the Christ Child), 9 inches, Cernit head and limbs, cloth body, one-of-a-kind

colored lights, and a huge blue spruce in the front yard was fully decorated."

Tucker was born on Christmas Day, so in addition to all the usual religious festivities, the family celebrated her birthday. "One year," she recalls, "my father—who was not among the handiest of men on the planet—spent weeks making a sugar-cube castle for me. He used pink icing to hold the 'bricks' together; it had turrets and archways and all manner of special features. Mom and Dad mounted it on a board and created a full display with a mirror pond for ice skaters, and sleighs and snowmen, and knights and damsels. It was beautiful, and I love it still, though it has long since vanished from existence," she says.

"Even today, some fifty years later, I decorate for Christmas. My husband just shakes his

Pepper Hume, King Kaspar, 15 inches (seated), Super Sculpey head, cloth body and limbs with wire armatures, one-of-a-kind

GIFTS FROM THE HEART

I remember sitting at the top of our stairs," says Penny Collins, "with my sisters and squinting at the sparkling lights on the Christmas tree. Baking and decorating cookies, caroling, how blessed we were. The nativity was always nestled under the tree and on Christmas Eve we would gather together to put Baby Jesus in the manger.

"My most wonderful memories, though, stem from when my own children were young and we kept Christmas quite simple. I remember the year we picked the perfect Christmas tree, and I 'sculpted' Christmas ornaments and a nativity from white bread and glue. My husband is a carpenter, and he made our son a barn and our daughter a doll cradle. I sewed a doll for my daughter, and matching clothes for her and the doll. I think I loved that Christmas the most because it was about gifts from the heart. Time, not money, was spent.

"The doll I made that year sprung a desire within me to keep creating dolls," Collins says. Today, her creations are a combination of clay and wood. "I have talked about making another nativity for years, a more permanent one," she says, but she put it off until recently, when she found a piece of wood that "looked like a camel to me. A little short and it lacked a complete face, but the camel was there waiting to be discovered." Atop the camel is one of the three kings. "The rest of the nativity figures will follow," she promises.

Penny Collins, Guide Us With Thy Perfect Light, 15 inches (on camel, 24 inches), Aves Apoxi Sculpt and polymer clay face, clay hands, cloth body, arms and legs, all with wire armatures, paperclay and Aves Apoxie Sculpt feet, one-of-a-kind

head and lets me go," Tucker adds. "We have lights and trees and Santas and nativities and elves and bells and wreaths and angels and anything else I can think of that catches my fancy. Each decoration has a memory, some quite old and some relatively recent, but they build more memories with each passing year."

In 1998, after years of creating unique decorations, Tucker turned to cloth dollmaking. Most of her original soft-sculpture pieces depict children, although among her early works were Santa Claus dolls. Memories of participating with her brother in Christmas pageants at her church inspired her twenty-piece nativity set shown on the opposite page.

While memories of childhood crèches inspire many of today's doll artists, it was the Christmas window display of a New York City department store that was the impetus for Pepper Hume's nativ-

Peter Wolf, *Holy Family*, 9-16 inches, Fimo heads and limbs, cloth and wire bodies, one-of-a-kind set

DID YOU KNOW?

During the French Revolution churches were looted and closed, and outdoor nativity scenes were banned. French families, wanting to keep the religious celebration of Christmas alive, began to create elaborate crèche scenes in their homes. The figures in these sets are called santons, a word that means "little saints" and dates back to the thirteenth century, when clay representations of the saints were made and sold throughout the country. The French nativity scenes included the Holy Family, magi, shepherds and angels, as well as representations of villagers bearing gifts for the newborn king. There were fishermen, bakers, cheese vendors, basket makers, wine merchants, farmers and so forth—often strongly resembling the local townspeople. Santons are still popular in France. Some are small, under-six-inch clay figures; others are larger, up to eighteen inches, have fabric clothing and carry miniature accessories, much like dolls.

Marilyn Bolden, *Our Lady of America*, 36 inches, porcelain head and limbs, cloth body, one-of-a-kind

Sandi Tucker,
Cherished Cherubs™
Children's Christmas
Pageant, 14 inches,
all cloth, limited
to 12 sets of Mary,
Joseph and Baby
Jesus, and 6 each of
the other 17 pieces

Alexander Doll
Company, Mary
and Joseph dolls, 8
inches, hard plastic,
open edition (dolls
are part of the
Nativity Set, shown)

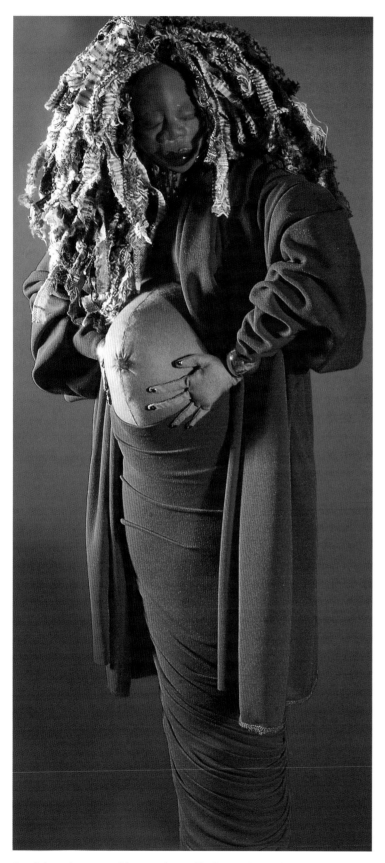

Patricia Coleman-Cobb, A Pocket Full of Miracles, polymer clay head, cloth body and limbs, one-of-a-kind

ity dolls. "The crèche comprised a huge, window-filling mountainside, richly populated with dolls portraying an entire medieval Italian village," she recalls. "I resolved to build my own crèche like it, if not quite so big."

The Texas artist began with King Melchior, which, surprisingly, was the first doll she'd ever made. This piece and the other magi, she notes, "are based on characters in Mennotti's *Amahl and the Night Visitors*, an opera I have costumed more than once. Like so many crèches, mine reflects more tradition and seasonal *joie de vivre* than historical accuracy.

"I have not quite kept up with my plan to add a doll each year," Hume admits, "but I have endeavored to keep expanding the environment to accommodate them. It's great fun to apply my experience as a designer of theatrical costumes and scenery to dolls and their environments. I picture Melchior as a man of great intelligence and dignity. A natural leader, he never needs to raise his voice, which is baritone in the opera." She sees Kaspar (shown on page 13) as a very old man who appears to be "lost in happy memories." Balthasar, she says, "is a mystery. . . His grim face suggests a warrior king, and his huge mink cape suggests great wealth."

German artist Peter Wolf brings his love for, and knowledge of, centuries of great European art to his Christmas creations. Among his designs are a Neapolitan-style Holy Family and a nativity set reflective of eighteenth-century art. Indeed, many of Wolf's creations are reminiscent of the decorative arts of earlier centuries, featuring rich colors, extensive use of gold and bronze, and fabulous fabrics, such as flowing silks and sumptuous brocades.

It is no easy task to sculpt figures based on the most celebrated story in the Bible. But the artists whose works appear here have succeeded in their objectives. Whether inspired by children's Christmas pageants, memories of crèche scenes from years past, yard and window displays, or great paintings and stained-glass depictions of the Holy Family, these dolls cut to the core of what the holiday is all about.

Judi L. Thompson,
Madonna and Child,
27 inches, cloth over
papier-mâché head,
cloth body and limbs,
one-of-a-kind

CHAPTER TWO

Angels

It came upon a midnight clear, that glorious song of old,
From angels bending near the earth, to touch their harps of gold.

NGELS PLAYED IMPORTANT ROLES throughout the Christmas story, mostly as messengers, giving assurance, bringing news and warning of danger. An angel appeared to Zacharias and told him that he and his wife Elizabeth would have a son, who they should name John, and that he would prepare the way for the Lord. An angel appeared to Mary and told her that she had found favor with God and would bear a son who would be called the Son of the God. An angel also appeared to Joseph, her fiancé, and said that he should not be afraid to wed Mary, "for that which is conceived in her is of the Holy Spirit. And she shall bring forth a son, and thou shalt call his name Jesus: for he shall save his people from their sins."

Angels also visited shepherds at the time of Christ's birth. First, a single angel appeared before a group camped in the fields with their sheep, saying, "Fear not: for behold, I bring you good tidings of great joy, which shall be to all people. For unto you is born this day in the city of David a Savior, which is Christ the Lord. And this

OPPOSITE PAGE, CLOCKWISE FROM TOP LEFT: **Rotraut Schrott**, Angel Annice, **29 inches, Cernit head and limbs, cloth body, one-of-a-kind**

Carole Piper, Angelica, **15 inches, Fimo head and limbs, cloth body with wire armature, one-of-a-kind**

Effanbee, Littlest Angel (Patsyette™), **9 inches, all vinyl, limited to an edition of 1,000**

Linda S. Kertzman, Losing My Halo! **Cernit and Super Sculpey head and limbs, cloth body, one-of-a-kind**

Helen Kish, Kish & Company, Angelic Riley, **8 inches, all vinyl, limited to an edition of 2,000**

"When I was a child, my mother and father always bought me the most beautiful dolls they could find," says Mazie Pannell of Anastasia's Dolls. "They almost always were large Madame Alexanders. How I loved them. Princess Elizabeth and Sonja Heine were two of my favorites. Also loved was a smaller doll—a Scarlett O'Hara—my last childhood doll.

"Many years later one of our grown daughters invited me to take a dollmaking class with her. I love any handwork, so I went—more to be with her than anything. Little did I know that fourteen years later I would be reminiscing about the wonderful years I have spent sculpting and making the dolls of my dreams—dolls that are inspired by the warm memories of my childhood doll friends.

"Anastasia's Dolls don't always have wings, but I always seek to give each an angelic look—delicate, pretty faces, silk and lace dresses, soft hair and accessories. The wings just add a finishing touch to some of them.

"Making dolls is the most exciting, satisfying and challenging thing that I have ever done," Pannell adds. The artist does all the sculpting, painting, and "putting together" of every Anastasia doll. Most of the Victorian-style dresses, however, are made by Toni Young. When these truly lovely costumes are complete, Pannell puts them on the dolls, and then has the fun of selecting and adding the accessories that complete each piece.

Anastasia's Dolls by Mazie Pannell, Sophie Angel and Angel Lucien, **28 and 30 inches respectively, porcelain heads and limbs, cloth bodies, limited to editions of 25 each**

Flo Hanover, Angel, **16 inches, Cernit head and limbs, cloth body with wire armature, one-of-a-kind**

shall be a sign unto you; ye shall find the babe wrapped in swaddling clothes, lying in a manger." Then a multitude of angels came into view, praising God and saying, "Glory to God in the highest, and on earth peace, good will toward men."

Still later, an angel appeared to Joseph and warned him that Herod would try to destroy the baby Jesus. In response, Joseph and Mary fled to Egypt, where they lived until another angel visited Joseph and told him that Herod was dead, and it was safe for them to return home.

Other angels are found throughout the Bible. In the very first book, Genesis, it is written that God placed cherubim at the entrance to the Garden of Eden, along with a flaming sword, to prevent Adam and Eve's return to Eden and the tree of life. Also in Genesis is the story of Lot, who was visited by two angels who warned him to take his wife and daughters out of the city of Sodom, which the Lord destroyed for the evil ways of its inhabitants. Perhaps the most vivid description of angels, however, is found in

ABOVE LEFT: **Elizabeth Jenkins**, Placing the Star, **20 inches (28 inches with base), all-La Doll (air-dried stone clay), one-of-a-kind**

ABOVE RIGHT: **Peter Wolf**, Angel Gabriel, **24 inches (with pedestal), Fimo head and limbs, cloth and wire body, one-of-a-kind**

LEFT: **Linda J. Kays**, The Oldest Angel, **16 inches, all resin, limited to an edition of 25**

DID YOU KNOW?

It's not Santa, but an angel who is believed to deliver Christmas gifts in some European countries. Children write Christmas letters to "little Jesus," and angels take them up to Him in heaven, then bring back the children's gifts. Hungarian and Polish children are told that not only does an angel deliver the presents, but this heavenly being also decorates the tree on Christmas Eve. Even nicer, before the angel leaves the home, it blesses all the children within.

Elizabeth Jenkins, Advent Angel, 27 inches, La Doll head, cloth arms, wooden shelves serve as legs, Etha foam and poly batting body, one-of-a-kind

the New Testament's last book: Revelations. There we find the report of the great battle in heaven between Michael and his angels and a great red dragon and his angels (Revelations 12:7-9). What awesome beings these angels are: terrifying in their anger and wondrous in their love.

According to biblical scholars, there are nine levels of angels. The highest are seraphim; guardians of God's throne, they have six wings. Two cover their faces, two cover their feet, and two are for flying. Next are the cherubim, who resemble human beings, but have two wings. After them come the thrones, who are angels of humanity, peace and submission; dominions, who are angels of leadership; virtues, the spirits of motion who control the elements; and powers, warrior angels who defend us from evil. The last three levels are archangels, who are most frequently mentioned in the Bible and who often serve as messengers; the principalities, beings created through Christ and for Him; and angels, who are the closest to human beings. The angels in this lowest level are considered the most caring. They carry our prayers to God, and God's answers and other messages to us. They have access to all other angels,

Bonnie Jones, Mother Angel, 19 inches, ProSculpt head, paperclay limbs and body with wire armatures, one-of-a-kind

SYMBOLS OF THE SEASON

When I was growing up," says Elizabeth Jenkins, "I had an aunt who sent me annual Advent calendars. They had little paper doors that were meant to be opened, one by one, as the days proceeded to Christmas. Behind each door was a picture or symbol of the story of this blessed season.

"My Advent Angel announces the coming of Christmas through similar symbols. This accounts for the stylized approach to the hair and costume. The style is part Elizabethan, part medieval, from that timeless otherworld where angels dwell."

In explaining this doll, Jenkins says, "The right hand shows the star that signaled the birth of Jesus, while the left hand shows the ascending dove, indicating the peaceful triumphant end of the story. The actual 'guiding star in the East' is a necklace worn by the angel.

"The mother and child," she notes, "are very simple figures shaped of felted wool fibers. The felted sheep symbolize not only the barnyard animals present at Jesus' birth, but the flock who have called him shepherd through all generations. The little drawer filled with straw reminds us of the humble manger, or a bird's nest with three eggs as symbols of the miracle of birth, and the eternal nature of hope."

Rita V. Webster, Rita's Art, Faith – Dressed as a Christmas Angel, 30 inches, porcelain head, hands and feet, cloth arms, legs and body, limited to an edition of 6 dolls, with one-of-a-kind outfits

ABOVE LEFT: Terry Antolick, My Idol, 14 inches, Super Sculpey head and limbs, cloth body with wire armature, one-of-a-kind

ABOVE: Judi L. Thompson, Kyle, 4½ inches, Super Sculpey head and arms, wired cloth legs and body, one-of-a-kind

and they assist anyone who asks for help.

"It is a difficult thing to personify an angel," notes Missouri artist Elizabeth Jenkins. "Through the centuries, artists have depicted these creatures by the dress and appearance that was the ideal beauty of the time. Creating a unique and timeless approach to the subject is harder than following images of the past, but it calls up creative resources within the artist that open new access channels for future creativity. Some might call this a true visit from the angel of inspiration."

Rather than looking to great paintings, ancient sculpture and stained-glass images of angels for ideas, many doll artists find inspiration for angel designs in the people dear to them. For instance, Terry Antolick says, "My grandmother inspired my doll titled My Idol; she was always so kind." The Ohio artist's mother was the stimulus for other designs. "She was the best seamstress and tried to teach me everything she knew," Antolick explains.

Judi L. Thompson, Collette, 17 inches, porcelain head and arms, cloth legs and body, one-of-a-kind

Gaby Rademann, Angel, 12½ inches (25 inches with base), porcelain head and limbs, porcelain and fabric body, one-of-a-kind

English artist Carole Piper gets joy and ideas for her little angels from her two grandchildren. "I look forward each Christmas to their school nativity play," she says. "The little ones always seem to be in a world of their own and wander about doing their own thing. Angelica (shown on page 19) is one of them!"

Being around tiny tots also spurs the talents of Judi L. Thompson. The Washington state dollmaker says Alisha, A Little Angel is a portrait of her grand-niece, "who at this age was an absolute angelic being." Thompson's Kyle (shown on page 24) was inspired by her neighbors' first grandchild—"such a happy little fellow," she says.

Sometimes, it's the face of the doll that causes the artist to give it wings. Such was the case with Flo Hanover's Angel (shown on page 20). "I sculpted the head as a demonstration piece," the Massachusetts artist says, adding: "Her youthful gaze came out as a surprise to me. She is so sweet and calm that I made her an angel, and have never sold her. She is on display in my studio with my favorite dolls."

At other times, something as simple as a piece of fabric inspires a doll. Bonnie Jones's Mother Angel, (shown on page 23) for instance, was inspired by a length of antique lace. "The lace has such a lovely, creamy, soft texture to it," says Jones, "that I could only envision an angel dressed in it." Inspiration for the doll's name, however, came "when I was painting her face: I realized she looked like my mother, who is now an angel in heaven."

Whatever the inspiration, dolls depicting angels make beautiful additions to the Christmas season, whether they're presented to others as loving gifts, or used to decorate one's home. An angel-topped tree, an angel in a wreath, or a group of angels on a mantle or tabletop all spread a message of love and peace.

Rotraut Schrott, Angel
Theresa, 32 inches, Cernit
head and limbs, cloth
body, one-of-a-kind

CHAPTER THREE

Santa Claus

Jolly Old Saint Nicholas, lean your ear this way,
Don't you tell a single soul what I'm going to say...

THE LEGEND OF A SECRET PURVEYOR OF GIFTS AT CHRISTMAS-time has evolved over many centuries, and the gift giver's name and, indeed, ideas about his appearance, are varied. Most everyone agrees, however, that the inspiration for this generous person—whom Americans call Santa Claus—comes from the Bishop of Myra (an area in what is now Turkey). Named Nicholas, he was born in the town of Patara and orphaned at an early age. He is said to have embraced the people of his village as his extended family, and used his inheritance to help those in need. He later became a bishop; renowned as a kind and generous man, he was also credited with performing many miracles. These included bringing children back to life, flying through the air to rescue a ship in distress and saving people from starvation by causing grain to multiply.

According to legend, he died on December 6, 343, and was buried in his church in Myra. Later, he was canonized by the church and became known as Saint Nicholas. He quickly became one of the Greek and Latin churches' most popular saints; in the sixth century, Emperor Justinian I built a church in his honor in Constantinople. Many diverse groups claimed him as their patron saint, including orphans, students, sailors, merchants, pawnbrokers and thieves.

The best-known story about Saint Nicholas concerns his generosity to three young women, the daughters of a poor man who considered selling one of the girls into slavery in order to attain dowries for the other two. The father's dilemma—whether to let all three girls

Trina Neher Ross, Original Artist Dolls, Santa's Helper, 12 inches, Li-qua-che head, hands and feet, fabric body with wire armature, limited edition of 10

CLOCKWISE FROM TOP LEFT: **Cindy Casper,** Hiatus, 14 inches, ProSculpt head and limbs, cloth body with wire armature

Maria Saracino, Making the List, 32 inches, Creal-Therm head, wire and fabric limbs, wood, wire and fabric body

Dave DeHoff, Santa, life size, ProSculpt head, cloth and wire limbs, welded-rod body

Tanya Abaimova, Santa With Toys, 11 1/2 inches (seated), ProSculpt head and limbs, cloth body with wire armature

Debra Parker Romero, Old World St. Nicks, Father Pierre, 30 inches, Super Sculpey head, cloth limbs, cloth-over-wire body

Glenda Bansmer, Saint Nicholas, 18 inches, ProSculpt head and limbs, fabric body with wire armature

Lori Varner, 'Twas the Night Before Christmas..., 19 inches, ProSculpt head and limbs, cloth body

Betty Lou Brynes, Silent Night, 25 inches, all ProSculpt PHOTO: J.P. BYRNES

All are one-of-a-kind.

Saint Nicholas was originally buried in Myra. However, in 1087, Italian merchants stole his body and moved it to Bari, Italy. Since then, the town has celebrated Saint Nicholas Day by putting a statue of him into a boat and sending it out into the Mediterranean Sea. Once it returns to land, the holiday festivities begin. His remains are still preserved in the church of San Nicola in Bari; up to the present day an oily substance, known as Manna di S. Nicola, which is highly valued for its medicinal powers, is said to flow from them.

LEFT: Judi L. Thompson, Mickey Rooney as Santa, 15 inches, Super Sculpey head and limbs, cloth and wire body, one-of-a-kind

BELOW: Lori Varner, High Aspirations, 21 inches, ProSculpt head and limbs, cloth body, one-of-a kind

suffer or to sacrifice one to benefit the others—moved the Bishop of Myra to help the family. In one version of this legend, he went to their home late one night and threw three bags of gold down the chimney. The sisters had washed their stockings that evening and hung them by the fire to dry. A bag of gold fell into one of each of the girls' socks—providing them with dowries and future generations with the tradition of hanging a Christmas stocking "by the fire with care, in hopes that Saint Nicholas soon will be there." In another version, as each of the three sisters was about to marry, the bishop threw gold through an open window and it landed in the girl's stocking or shoe.

Saint Nicholas's name day is December 6th, commemorating the day of his death. It has been celebrated for centuries, often with gifts. For instance, in the Middle Ages (circa 500-1500), on the eve of Saint Nicholas Day, children would put out food for the bishop, straw for his horse and a strong drink for his attendant. The next day, good boys and girls would find toys and candy in exchange for their offerings. Bad children would find their offerings untouched, except for the addition of a rod or whip.

With the Protestant Reformation of the sixteenth century, which challenged the Catholic Church and the universal authority of the Pope, the veneration of Catholic saints was banned in many areas of Europe. Still, the custom of giving gifts in

Candace Rush, Father Christmas, 18 inches, ProSculpt head and limbs, cloth body, one-of-a-kind

Margaret Mousa, Mr. Kringle, 36 inches, porcelain head and limbs, cloth body with armature, one-of-a-kind

Marlene Kawalez, Woodland Santa, 14 inches (sitting), ProSculpt head and arms, paperclay boots, cloth body with wire armature, one-of-a-kind

December was popular, and became part of the Christmas holiday celebration, rather than of Saint Nicholas Day. After all, the three kings, or magi, brought gifts to the Christ child, so it wasn't inappropriate to include the exchange of gifts during the Christmas season.

In many areas, Saint Nicholas was transformed from a religious figure to a secular one. In France, for example, people began celebrating visits by Père Noël, who left gifts in shoes. In Germany, the gift giver was called Weihnachtsmann; in England, gifts were distributed by Father Christmas, who was depicted as a large man wearing scarlet robes. In Russia, Saint Nicholas evolved into the secular Father Frost, who distributed gifts to children on New Year's Eve.

In Holland, however, children still looked forward to visits from Sinterklass. He continued to be depicted as a bishop, dressed in a red robe and miter, carrying a staff and riding a stately white horse. His assistant, whom the Dutch called Black Peter, assuming he would be covered with soot, did the difficult work of delivering the gifts. Later, the appearance of Sinterklass evolved into that of a typical seventeenth-century Dutchman, complete with pipe.

While European immigrants all brought their own customs to America, the American celebra-

MYRA'S BISHOP: A SANTA OF HER OWN

"When I was a child, my grandmother spent the Christmas season with us each year. It was a magical time for me," says Myra Sherrod.

"During one of her early visits, she gave me a book about the legends of Santa Claus, and every evening before bedtime, she would read a chapter to me. Imagine my delight when I learned that St. Nicholas, the very first Santa Claus, was the Bishop of Myra. I loved hearing of the many miracles he supposedly performed. He was such a marvelous fellow—the Bishop of Myra! My own personal saint! Not many kids could lay claim to anything like that, and I felt decidedly special," she remembers.

"My grandmother—who shared my love of dolls— also gave me a book about dollmaking patterns for simple cloth dolls. Together, we'd create whole families from the guidelines. They must have been incredibly crude, but I remember thinking they were wonderful.

"In my eighth year, as the Christmas season drew near, I was looking at my Santa Claus book and had an idea: My grandmother and I would make Santa dolls and decorate the house with them. My grandmother, whose imagination equaled my own, thought it was a wonderful idea. By Christmas we had a nice little collection of dolls. I was so proud of what we'd done and many years later, the memory of it still shines bright.

"Although my first Santa book disappeared, as did those first dolls, I have not forgotten its marvelous illustrations and draw them forth from my memory as inspiration for my current Christmas dollmaking.

"And that first book about dollmaking? I still have it, and occasionally thumb through it. Doing so takes me back to that happy time long ago when a little girl and her grandmother wrought their own Santa Claus miracle."

Myra Sherrod, Born Yesterday Art Dolls, Inc., St. Nicholas, the Bishop of Myra, 24 inches, Cernit head and limbs, cloth body with wire armature, one-of-a-kind

TOP: **Nancy Di Ponte,** A Gift from Santa, girl: 10 inches, Santa: 18 inches, polymer-clay heads and limbs, cloth bodies with wire armatures, one-of-a-kind set

ABOVE: **Elizabeth Jenkins,** King Wenceslaus, 32 inches, paperclay head and arms, foam body with batting and wooden shelves, one-of-a-kind

TOP: **Marlene Kawalez,** Santa's Helper, 15 inches, ProSculpt head and limbs, cloth body with wire armature, one-of-a-kind

ABOVE: **Debra Parker Romero,** Old World St. Nicks, Frank C. Seaside Santa, 32 inches, Super Sculpey head, cloth limbs, cloth body over wire and steel rods, one-of-a-kind

TOP: **Myra Sherrod,** Born Yesterday Art Dolls, Inc., Civil War Santa, 24 inches, Puppen Fimo head and limbs, cloth body with wire armature, one-of-a-kind

ABOVE: **Nancy Di Ponte,** Father Christmas, 18 inches, polymer-clay head and limbs, cloth body with wire armature, one-of-a-kind

Maria Saracino, *Runaway Sled II*, 18 inches, ProSculpt head, wire and fabric limbs, wood, wire and fabric body, one-of-a-kind

tion of Christmas, with visits from Santa Claus (notice how similar his name is to the Dutch Sinterklass), was mostly due to the influence of the concentrated population of Dutch in New York. It was New Yorkers who also gave the American Santa his early personality.

In 1809, Washington Irving—the American essayist, novelist and historian—published a satirical novel titled *A History of New York from the Beginning of the New World to the End of the Dutch Dynasty*, which he wrote under the pseudonym of Diedrich Knickerbocker. This book, which makes fun of New York's Dutch past, describes Saint Nicholas as wearing traditional Dutch clothing, flying over rooftops and dropping presents down chimneys. In an 1812 revision of the book, Irving has him riding to the rooftops in a red wagon. Interestingly, Irving makes no reference to Black Peter, and this character has never become a part of American folklore.

About a dozen years later, another New York writer added considerably to the legend of Santa Claus—turning him into a fat, jolly elf. Clement Clark Moore, whose father was the president of Columbia College and who himself was a classics professor at New York's General Theological Seminary, wrote a Christmas poem for his six children. Titled "A Visit from Saint Nicholas" (now known as "The Night Before Christmas"), it delighted all who heard it. Friends encouraged Moore to publish it, but he refused, so a relative secretly

Maria Saracino, *Making the List*, 16 inches, ProSculpt head, wire and fabric limbs, wood, wire and fabric body, one-of-a-kind

Jack Johnston, Mandolin Master, 15 inches, all ProSculpt, one-of-a-kind

BELOW: Jack Johnston, Teddy Bear Maker Stocking Up for Christmas, 18 inches, all ProSculpt, one-of-a-kind

A GIFT OF LIFE

Santa Claus is very close to the heart of artist, author and dollmaking instructor Jack Johnston. In December 1982, "we invited Santa Claus (my father) to our home," says Johnston. "He put each of our six children on his lap to ask what they wanted for Christmas. When he interviewed Ethan (our five-year-old), he noticed his coloring wasn't normal, and that he had fresh bruises on his arms and face. He recommended we take him to the doctor immediately.

"We took Ethan straight to the emergency room, and within an hour he was diagnosed with leukemia. We had to face the fact that Ethan would likely not make it to see another Christmas. He went through chemotherapy, and radiation treatment for that full year. One year passed, then two, and eventually, five. We couldn't afford the treatments, but fortunately The Children's Miracle Network helped. Finally, Ethan was found to be cancer free, and he has gone on to live a happy and normal life," says the artist. "So you can see why Santa, The Children's Miracle Network and Christmas have, and always will have a very special place in the Johnston family's home and hearts."

The magic of Christmas begins for dollmaker Glenda Bansmer with what she calls "an urgency for activity. When I was a child, there were always things that had to be started or completed to make the Christmas season as splendid as possible," she recalls.

"We lived in a rural area, which seemed to reinforce the need to prepare for Christmas. After the bounty of the fields had been gathered in the fall, we prepared to share portions of it, such as walnuts, canned fruits and preserves, which had to be made. My mother, who was an accomplished homemaker and seamstress, also spent time searching for just the right fabrics, ribbons and other items needed to make the holidays special. Her joyous efforts for adding just the right decorative touch, and in planning and preparing an elegant Christmas meal helped build anticipation for the arrival of Christmas Day in all of us. Because of her, the colors, sounds and smells of Christmas have always filled my soul.

"My father always loved the excitement and joy of the Christmas season, too. Some of his special gifts included wooden animals that he cut out and my mother decorated, a large sled that he pulled behind the tractor when the season brought snow, and an endless supply of firewood that he loved to burn in our large fireplace. How fondly I remember those occasions when there would be peals of laughter from family and friends, and hurried action on Dad's part to get the damper open after a fire had been started. We'd merrily throw open the windows and doors to clear the house of smoke.

"What fun it is to reflect on the meaning of the season and the shared love that has always been part of my holidays," says Bansmer. "I have inherited the values, emotions and love of Christmas from my family, and I take pride in my efforts to pass these values on to my daughters and grandchildren. Along the way, I have developed skills that have enabled me to bring my own special gifts to the holiday season: the dolls that I make. My hope is that my Santas and other Christmas dolls will enhance the joy of my family members and others, stirring warm memories of holidays past and dreams of those to come."

sent it to an out-of-town paper, the *Troy Sentinel*, which printed it in its Christmas Eve 1823 edition. "A Visit from Saint Nicholas" was such a hit that it quickly received wide publication.

Moore's Santa Claus was inspired, in part, by Irving's description of him as a stout, pipe-smoking Dutchman clad, typically, in a red coat with a thick belt and leather boots. Also believed to have influenced Moore's poem was "The Children's Friend," a Christmas poem published a year earlier; it contains the first known reference to Santa's sleigh and reindeer.

The next rendition of Santa Claus came from an artist: Thomas Nast, a caricaturist for *Harper's Weekly*. A German immigrant, he created illustrations of Santa for the magazine each December from 1863 through 1886. He is credited for giving Santa his North Pole address.

Some years later, another commercial illustrator, Haddon Sund-

TOP: **Glenda Bansmer,** All I Want for Christmas, **14 inches, ProSculpt head and limbs, fabric body with wire armature, one-of-a-kind**

ABOVE: **Glenda Bansmer,** Father Christmas, **23 inches, ProSculpt head and limbs, fabric body with wire armature, one-of-a-kind**

FROM TOP: **Jack Johnston,** The Master Teddy Bear Maker & Elf, **15 inches, all ProSculpt, one-of-a-kind. Ronna Morse,** Meeting Santa, **Santa: 7 inches, children: 4 inches, all polymer clay, one-of-a-kind set. Betsey P. Baker,** St. Nicholas and Pete, **15 inches (mounted), Super Sculpey head and limbs, cloth body with wire armature (the horse is papiermâché over a wire armature)**

blom, gave us what remains the most universal image of Santa. He was hired by the Coca-Cola Company to create an ad campaign featuring Santa drinking a Coke, in an effort to sell it as a winter drink, as well as a summer thirst quencher. (It is difficult today to envision a time when carbonated beverages weren't year-round drinks.) Sundblom's first Coca-Cola Santa illustration was published in the 1931 *Saturday Evening Post.* The artist continued to create Santa illustrations for Coca-Cola advertisements until 1964.

Since then, many artists, including the dollmakers whose works are featured here, have provided us with delightful images of Santa Claus. Some doll artists find inspiration for their creations in old books. Betsey P. Baker, for instance, based her St. Nicholas and Pete doll on an old Dutch children's book. "I sold the book with the doll, so I can't be more specific about its title," she notes with regret. The Santa is mounted on a horse, also made by the artist, and wears a red wool hat and cape, lined with gold satin, and a white silk robe; Pete is costumed in brown velveteen and holds a bag of toys.

Some base their designs on historic figures, such as the Bishop of Myra, or the tenth-century Bohemian King Wenceslaus—whose name was made famous by a 130-year-old Christmas carol. Elizabeth Jenkins created a doll of Good King Wenceslaus (shown on page 34) because, she says, "He personifies the spirit of generosity and hospitality. The first Christian Saint of Bohemia, he chose to celebrate his faith by giving food, drink and coins to those who lived in his kingdom." The artist's King Wenceslaus is a shelf doll, meant to be placed

ALL I WANT FOR CHRISTMAS

When dollmaker Betty Lou Byrnes thinks of childhood holidays, she remembers a Christmas when she knew exactly what she wanted from Santa. "I had seen a doll in a magazine that I instantly fell in love with and so hoped that Santa would bring to me on Christmas Day," she says. "I showed the magazine picture to my mother, who said the doll was too expensive for Santa to bring, because he had a lot of children to give presents to. I thought about that, and was very sad that I wouldn't get the doll. Then I thought of a plan to help Santa get it for me. I told my mother that to help pay for the doll I would give Santa all of the money I had earned doing chores. She said maybe that would work. So I left my savings for him, along with his milk and cookies, on Christmas Eve.

"Christmas morning was everything I'd dreamed it would be. Santa had delivered that special doll I had seen in the magazine; I cherished it for years and to this day fondly remember my Sparkle Plenty doll," Byrnes says.

"From that day on, Santa has been someone special in my life. I will always love Santa, and I try to express that love and the kindness he represents in my Santa art dolls."

Pauline Flaga, Cuisine 'Art' Elf, 23 inches, ProSculpt head and limbs, cloth body, one-of-a-kind

Linda S. Kertzman, Santa's Little Angels, 18 inches (sitting), Santa: Cernit and Super Sculpey head and limbs, cloth body with wire armature, Angels: all Cernit-Super Sculpey mix, one-of-a-kind

SHARING THE MAGIC

"The smells and the tastes of childhood Christmases come back to me so clearly when I work on my Christmas creations," says doll artist Linda Kertzman.

"When I was a child, the days leading up to Christmas were the most wonderful of the year. The smell of gingerbread coming from my grandmother's kitchen, along with the jams and jellies and bread. My grandmother's bread was the best of all. It came from the oven lightly browned, crusted, high and puffy with steam.

"I also loved it when my Mom decided to bake. She didn't always follow recipes, and sometimes she made up her own totally. She'd put the radio on with all the favorite Christmas carols, and bring out our old, somewhat-bent tin cookie cutters from the pantry. We'd use them every year, but made up our own silly shapes, too. We'd bend the arm of an angel to wave hello, and form a sleigh into a more elongated and elegant shape than the original mold. We used the tiny leftovers to form faces on the sleighs or wreaths for our angels. I guess my first sculpting was with cookie dough!

"There was always one day that Mom and Dad took us Christmas shopping and to see Santa. I have three brothers and one sister. My Santa's Little Angels (shown on opposite page) reminds me of this time. The Santa of my youth was all cuddly and velvet and large and red, and he had a deep voice and seemed filled with love. His wife, Mrs. Claus, was a small, white-haired woman who just smiled and patted us on the head and wished us a Merry Christmas as we left to shop for toys and gifts for each other.

"My favorite present was always my Christmas doll. Everything else seems to fade, but I can still see those oblong boxes waiting beneath the tall trees. I remember Tiny Tears and Ginny dolls, Baby Dear and Patti Playpal. The smell of a new doll and the smells of pine and fresh oranges can send me right back under those trees we cut down and dragged home so many years ago.

"I was very blessed to have a loving family, a grandmother who lived with us, and brothers and a sister. Memories of my childhood with them are some of my very best memories, and I cherish them and try to share them with my children and grandchildren. Life isn't always easy, but these memories are my little 'pockets of peace,' and because I had such moments, I can carry the magic in my heart, and hopefully always share the magic!"

Mark Dennis, Bears Away, 28 inches, ProSculpt head and limbs, cloth body, one-of-a-kind

in a home's entrance hall as a symbol of hospitality. "The shelves in its base contain small favors for holiday visitors," the dollmaker explains.

Jan Coe's Wenceslas Santa (which graces the cover of this book and page 45) was inspired by the "musical story" of the king's good works. "When I was a girl, I would sit at the piano and play and sing this song by the light of the Christmas tree. I can still sing every verse from memory. Singing this and all my other favorite Christmas songs every evening while my parents cleaned up the kitchen was a big part of the magic of Christmas." About her Wenceslas Santa, she says, "This doll actually started out as the good king, then evolved into a Father Christmas figure. He is carrying both food and gifts in his bag."

Other doll artists, like Nanci Di Ponte, find inspiration in old photographs. "I love looking at old photos of Christmases past," says Di Ponte. "They awaken memories of my own childhood Christ-

Bonnie Jones, White Mink Santa, 29 inches, ProSculpt head, clay hands and feet, cloth limbs and body with wire armatures, one-of-a-kind

CINDY CASPER'S BLUE LIGHT SPECIAL

Cindy Casper, The Toy Maker, 20 inches, Super Sculpey head and limbs, cloth body with wire armature, one-of-a-kind

Memories really do affect the way we sculpt," says dollmaker Cindy Casper, who shares this one of a Christmas past. "My grandfather, whom we called Poppy, and I were doing some last-minute Christmas shopping, when an announcement came over the store's loud speaker: 'Aluminum Christmas trees now only fifty cents at the flashing blue light while supply lasts.' I looked up at Poppy and don't know if he saw the excitement in my eyes, or if I saw excitement in his, but the next thing I knew, we were hurrying toward the flashing blue light to stake out our prize: a fifty-cent, four-foot silver aluminum Christmas tree. I was so excited I couldn't believe our good fortune. Now I had a surprise for my Mom and Dad.

"At home, the tree was set up on our closed-in front porch. I'm not sure if my dear mother shared my enthusiasm for it. I do know that, as excited as I was, she would never let on if she didn't. It was, as all aluminum trees are, rather gaudy, but at eight years old, I thought it was the most beautiful thing I had ever seen.

"That was more than forty years ago. The other day, my husband and I were going through a flea market and there in one of the stands was an old aluminum tree. I couldn't get over the way the sight of that old tree transported me back to a precious moment when my Poppy, with his rosy cheeks, twinkling eyes and deep voice, took a little eight-year-old girl and hurried through a store to find that blue-light special.

"As an adult looking back, I think Poppy saw the beam in my eye, and knew that having one of these trees would make me happy. I hadn't thought about it until I saw this flea-market tree, but my Santas have the same qualities in them that my dear dad and my Poppy had: sparkling eyes, rosy cheeks and a love for making people smile, especially their children and grandchildren. Perhaps that's why family friends say to me, 'Hey, that Santa reminds me of your dad—or is it your Poppy?'"

mases, so full of joyous expectation of all that the holiday holds. In this world of ever-changing, uncertain times, we need to look back to the traditions of the past in order to find the courage and hope that we need to meet the years ahead," she adds.

Lori Varner finds inspiration in her brother-in-law's Norwegian roots (her Julenisse is based on that country's traditional holiday gift giver), old Christmas cards and old photos. Her Twas the Night Before Christmas (shown on page 29) was the result of memories evoked by photo of herself, taken when she was a little girl. In it, she says, "I'm in pajamas with a matching nightcap, reading 'Twas the Night Before Christmas' as I lay in bed, my face as red as a tomato, from the childhood sickness called scarlatina." She'd always loved the idea of Santa

BELOW: **Lori Varner,** Amber's Surprise, **Santa: 20 inches, Amber: 16 inches, ProSculpt heads and limbs, cloth bodies, one-of-a-kind**

RIGHT, FROM TOP: **Käthe Kruse Puppen GmbH/Europlay Corp.,** Niklas, **21 inches, composition head, cloth body and limbs stuffed with reindeer hair, limited to an edition of 40**

Barbara Scully, Santa the Collector, **29 inches, ProSculpt head, cloth and wire arms and body, one-of-a-kind**

Lori Varner, The Norwegian Santa 'Julenisse,' **18 inches, ProSculpt head and limbs, cloth body, one-of-a-kind**

Tanya Abaimova, Santa's Checklist, **5 inches (seated), all Fimo, one-of-a-kind**

Jan Coe, Does This Make Me Look Fat? 19 inches, polymer-clay head and limbs, cloth body with wire armature, one-of-a-kind

A DEPARTMENT STORE SANTA

More than 150 years ago—way back in 1841—a Kriss Kringle character first appeared at J.W. Parkinson's Philadelphia store during the Christmas season. Since then, Santa has visited thousands of stores and heard millions of secret wishes. Doll artist Jan Coe takes us behind the department-story Santa scenes with Does This Make Me Look Fat? The older gentleman in this piece, the artist explains, "looks forward every year to talking with the children and hearing their wishes for Santa. He has the hair and glasses down pat, but has to add the beard and a little extra padding to get his costume just right."

"As a girl," she says, "my favorite Christmas tradition was going to see Santa at the shopping mall. Eventually I asked my mother how Santa could be in so many places at once. She explained that the department-store Santas were Santa's elves, helping him find out what all the children wanted for Christmas while he toiled away at the North Pole. I guess this explanation worked," Coe adds, "because she eventually had to explain the whole affair to me years later. Otherwise, I think I would still believe. If the truth be told, I guess I really still do."

placing "his finger aside of his nose and giving a nod, up the chimney he rose."

Most of the other artists whose work is represented here also find inspiration from memories of childhood holidays. As Bonnie Jones tells us, "The traditions my family celebrated at Christmas were very warm and cozy and heartfelt. My father was the one who really wanted my sister and me to believe in Santa Claus forever. Each Christmas Eve he'd read to us the memorable 'Twas the Night Before Christmas,' and I promise you, I always heard those reindeer hoofs on the roof and a faint tinkle of bells."

Each year, Jones says, her hometown newspaper would publish the famous "Yes, Virginia, there is a Santa Claus. He exists as certainly as love and generosity and devotion exist…" editorial that was written by Francis P. Church for the New York Sun in 1897, in response to a letter from eight-year-old Virginia O'Hanlon. This, too, Jones's father would read to her and her siblings each Christmas Eve.

The Christmas memories that Jones holds closest to her heart, however, are of their formal dinners. "We always had someone at our home who had no family in the area with whom to celebrate the season. It was always a special occasion, with my father standing at the head of the table and, with great ceremony, carving the turkey. I remember my father's love of the season more than anything, and how he passed that on to us. We, in turn, have passed it on to our children. So my love for creating Santa Claus in figurative sculptures definitely comes from my childhood," she adds.

English artist Margaret Mousa's work is inspired by a strong memory of an early Christmas. "I remember long ago, I would have been no more than four years old, a particularly special Christmas," she says. "From great adversity came one of the most meaningful memories of my life. In the midst of an especially bitter Cornish winter, I had succumbed to the harsh conditions; the long English winter had left me ill and quite sad. Christmas was just around the corner, and I remember wondering if Santa was going to visit that year, as the storms were fierce. In an effort to cheer me up, my mother bought a beautiful doll, which she crafted into an angel for the top of our tree. She sat by the firelight and sewed through the night, fashioning the most amazing dresses for her.

"My mother had told me that Christmas was special," Mousa continues, "and that through the sadness and the sickness that I was suffering good things would come— and they did, with the angel at the top of our tree. Indeed, Santa had made his way through the snow and the wind to deliver a Christmas of beautiful memories. And so, in keeping with tradition, I have harnessed that valuable childhood memory and used it to craft an old-style Santa—just as my mother had made our angel many years ago—and so the message lives on: Christmas is special."

Jan Coe, Wenceslas Santa, 20 inches, polymer-clay head and limbs, foam body over wire armature, one-of-a-kind

CHAPTER FOUR

Christmas Kids

Jolly old Saint Nicholas, lean your ear this way,
Don't you tell a single soul what I'm going to say...

Effanbee Doll Company, Merry Moments (Patsyette™), 9 inches, all vinyl, limited to an edition of 1,000

EW, IF ANY, DOLL COLLECTORS CAN LOOK AT A LITTLE DOLL dressed for the holidays and not remember a favorite Christmas present of the past—a delightful doll that became a best friend and confidante. The dolls shown here—a delectable group of turn-of-the-twenty-first-century Christmas kids—were all made with loving care, and put into their very best outfits for special delivery by Santa. Some of them may have found their way under your tree, or perhaps brought comfort and joy to your children or grandchildren.

Personal experiences, favorite playmates of the past, family traditions and the customs of their countries all provide inspiration for today's doll designers and makers. For example, Norwegian artist Sissel Bjorstad Skille notes, "It has always been a tradition in Norway to wear one's best clothes on Christmas Eve, which is the height of Christmas celebrations in my country. The national costumes are still used on such occasions in many places." Thus she has dressed some of her Christmas cuties in just such costumes. Skille's Elisabeth (shown on page 59), for example, displays a costume from Hallingdal. Making her extra special, Skille has given this doll her own tiny Christmas tree with, explains the artist, "tiny copies of ornaments from my childhood, made by me."

Stacia McDonough, who uses only her first name on the designs for her company, Neva Dolls, is an American, but all of her dolls are made in Russia and display the rich traditional costumes of that country. As she explains, she developed a love for dolls and a passion for Russia during her childhood.

Stacia grew up in a home that resembled an "extraordinary museum," she says. "My mother, Donna, was an antiques dealer with an eye for the finer things of life. She was a collector of old French

Angela and John Barker, Sophie, 33 inches (left), porcelain head and arms, composition legs and body, Georgina, 31 inches, porcelain head and arms, composition legs and body, each limited to an edition of 15

ABOVE: **Käthe Kruse Puppen GmbH/Europlay Corp.,** Claire, 14 inches, composition head, stock-inette over sculpted foam body and limbs, limited to an edition of 30

ABOVE RIGHT: **Lee Middleton Original Dolls,** Waiting for Santa, 21 inches, vinyl head and limbs, cloth body, two versions – white doll is limited to an edition of 700, the black doll is limited to an edition of 300

RIGHT: **Lee Middleton Original Dolls,** Cookies for Santa, 21 inches, vinyl head and limbs, cloth body, limited edition of 900

OPPOSITE PAGE: **Flo Hanover,** Brandon, 13 1/2 inches (seated), Cernit head and limbs, cloth body with wire armature, one-of-a-kind

and German dolls. My father, Louis Manzo, was an international businessman and always traveled to exotic destinations. Dad always brought home the most remarkable dolls from around the globe. My favorite was a little rag doll he got for me in Guatemala. I absolutely adored this little girl and slept with her every night.

"One special Christmas, fate stepped in and Santa brought me a little ballerina jewelry box," Stacia remembers. "When you lifted the lid, the ballerina began to twirl to the dreamy melody of 'Lara's Theme,' from the movie *Dr. Zhivago*. From that moment on, I was enamoured by the Russian culture."

The artist is an avid reader who holds a degree in literature from Monmouth University. "I took many art classes and always had a passion for period couture. Hence, the splendid bouquet of the arts: fashion, literature, Russian history and my love of dolls—all of these forces just united and thus my foray into doll crafting began.

"My inspirations for Neva Dolls," she adds, "come from the essence of Russia: the elaborate Russian architecture, the rich history, the fun-

GERMAN CELEBRATIONS

Northern and southern Germans have slightly different holiday traditions, but both get their gifts on Christmas Eve, which for children is the most important time, says doll artist Gaby Rademann. "I'm from Berlin," she says, "and as a child I always expected Father Christmas to come between 5 and 6 p.m. and to bring us all our gifts. Father Christmas is very important for German children. He has a big book with bad and good things that the kids did during the past year—but there are always a few more good things than bad, which is the reason the children get gifts. While waiting for Father Christmas, we would sit together around our Christmas tree, filled with Christmas balls, figurines, little wood-carved figures and toys, and sing Christmas songs. After the *Bescherung*, we'd have dinner and a quiet—but not too quiet—party.

"In the south," she says, "Germans begin celebrating weeks before Christmas by attending the Christmas Markets around Bavaria. In Munich, we have the traditional *Christkindlmarkt*. Late in the afternoon, we meet our friends on the famous Marienplatz, have a *Glühwein*, because it is very cold, and then visit the outdoor booths. They are filled with traditional Christmas gift items—mostly made in China, like in the U.S.—but also very typical things made in little Austrian and Bavarian villages and valleys in the Alps. There are bands dressed in Bavarian outfits, playing traditional Bavarian Christmas music that adds to the magic. It is very peaceful and we all get the feeling that 'we shall overcome....'

"On Christmas Eve, southern children wait for the arrival of the *Christkindl*, who brings their gifts. Then they, too, enjoy a special meal and party.

"Throughout Germany," Rademann says, "We wish our friends and neighbors a *Frohliche Weihnachten and einen guten Rutsch in Neuew Jahr* (health and good luck for the New Year)."

The first Christmas card was produced in Britain the same year that Charles Dickens' *A Christmas Carol* was published: 1843. The two men responsible were Sir Henry Cole (1808-1882) and John Callcott Horsley (1817-1903). Cole wanted to urge his friends to be more generous to the destitute during the holiday season, and didn't have time to write lengthy letters to them. He asked Horsley to create artwork for a card depicting the feeding and clothing of the poor.

Sir Henry studied watercolor and drawing and became an industrial designer and a museum director. He organized England's Great Exhibition of 1851, and, due in part to its success, became the first director of the South Kensington Museum (renamed the Victoria and Albert in 1899).

Horsley created a charming illustration featuring a family embracing each other, sipping wine and generally having a grand old time. The inclusion of the wine was unfortunate, for 1843 was also the year that England's National Temperance Society was founded. Because one of the children in Horsley's illustration is being given a sip of wine, members of the new-formed society were up in arms. They blasted the card as fostering the moral corruption of children.

Printed on the card was "A Merry Christmas and a Happy New Year to You." One thousand cards were produced, and they were priced at one penny each. How many of these cards Sir Henry sent is unknown, and it is believed that he sent no cards the following year. But perhaps because of the publicity the card got, the custom took hold, and people have been sending cards to family and friends ever since.

As for Horsley, in his obituary, published in the October 20, 1903, issue of *The Times* newspaper of London, he is credited with being "one of the best 'subject painters' of his day." The author also noted that Horsley was "one of the most sweet-tempered of men, and one of the most innocent." This was mentioned because late in his life, Horsley led a campaign against "the nude in art." For this, he was held up to considerable public ridicule and dubbed "Clothes" Horsley.

The sending of Christmas cards became popular in America, even though initially the cards had to be imported from England. The first American-printed holiday cards were issued in 1860 by a German immigrant and lithographer, Louis Prang. Perhaps the most historic Christmas card is the one commissioned by Abraham Lincoln during the Civil War. In an effort to boost morale, President Lincoln asked political cartoonist and illustrator Thomas Nast to create a card featuring Santa Claus with Union troops.

OPPOSITE PAGE, LEFT: **Beverly Stoehr**, **Paradise Galleries**, Miss Gingerbread and Master Gingerbread, 23 inches, porcelain heads and arms, cloth legs and bodies, limited to editions of 100,000 each

OPPOSITE, BELOW LEFT: **Seymour Mann, Inc.**, A Christmas Stocking, 12 inches, porcelain head and limbs, cloth body, limited to an edition of 350

BELOW: **Linda Mason**, **Paradise Galleries**, Christmas Sparkle, 14 inches, porcelain head and limbs, cloth body, limited to an edition of 100,000

CANADA'S WINTER WONDERLAND

The winters may be frigid in Canada, but heavy snows beckon children outdoors. Thus it's not surprising that sleds and ice skates figure high on Canadian children's gift lists, and that they're also favorite accessories for Christmas dolls.

As Ontario artist Marlene Kawalez notes, "One of my favorite pastimes was frolicking and sledding over fresh-fallen snow. The play would come to an end only when my fingers and toes got frozen from the snow." The artist also enjoyed ice-skating—but says she spent most of that time with her "knees and bum on the ice—and searching for winterland fairies.

"During the magical time at Christmas," she says, "if you venture out to the woodlands you may be fortunate enough to get a glimpse of something special. Among the trees and snow-covered branches can be seen fairies busily decorating their own tiny trees. Santa visits all creatures great and small."

Marlene Kawalez, The Skater, 16 inches, ProSculpt head and arms, wire and cloth legs, cloth body with wire armature, one-of-a-kind

loving people and the vast landscape. I absorb it all while I am there. The entire culture floods my soul; it gets processed and then turned into my dolls."

Winters in Texas, where Ann Myatt creates her Just Like Me dolls, are a far cry from those of her childhoods in Michagan. So Myatt reaches back into her memories for inspiration for her Christmas dolls. "I can remember Christmas Eves when fluffy white flakes would fall, leaving clean, virginal snow scenes to gaze at on Christmas morning, while we were inside, toasty and warm," she explains. "It is magical when that happens, so you can imagine the excitement in Texas in 2004 when it actually snowed on Christmas Eve. I was in my car when it started, and you could count the individual flakes. All the drivers rolled down their windows to let the flakes fall on their hands. The sense of joy was tangible."

Remembering the simple pleasures of Christmas snows, Myatt created White Christmas (shown on page 62), featuring a little girl secure in her hood and cape, which the artist describes as "carefree in the cold, and probably off to visit her grandmother, or maybe on her way to church." Another Myatt doll, Christmas Concert, stems from memories of her early years in Catholic school. "We had a Christmas pageant each year, and I can still remember the smell of the angel costumes and the heat from the stage lights. My little Amy with her violin, about to perform at her Christmas concert, brings back memories of that time."

Like Myatt's Christmas Concert doll, which has her own violin, and Skille's Elisabeth (shown on page 59), with her own tiny tree, many of the other holiday darlings shown here have charming accessories. The Alexander Doll Company's Peppermint Swirl (shown on page 57), for example, comes

ABOVE LEFT: Margie Herrera, Helen– A Scottish Lass, 20 inches, porcelain head and limbs, cloth body, limited to an edition of 5

ABOVE: Adriana Rovina Innaciotti, Christmas, 22 inches, Cernit head and limbs, cloth body, one-of-a-kind

LEFT: Adriana Rovina Innaciotti, É Arrivata S. Lucia, 24 inches, Cernit heads and limbs, cloth bodies, one-of-a-kinds

In Russia, where Neva Dolls are made, Father Frost takes the role of Western countries' Santa Claus. He is almost always accompanied by his granddaughter, Snow Girl. The dolls that children get from Father Frost often depict characters from old Russian fairy tales, such as *The Frog Princess*. Stacia, the designer of Neva Dolls' porcelain creations, has found inspiration from these tales, too.

The Frog Princess story, she says, is about a Russian czar looking for wives for his three sons. The boys shoot arrows into the sky and, according to the story, where the arrows land they will find their wives. It works for the first two brothers, but the youngest, Ivan, finds his arrow in the mouth of a bullfrog. He asks for the arrow back, but the frog insists that she is his bride-to-be. Ivan takes the frog back to the palace,

where he receives considerable kidding. But at the tale's end, the frog transforms into the most beautiful woman in the land; she and Ivan marry and live happily ever after.

Stacia, an American who became interested in Russian dolls after receiving one as a gift from her father, finds inspiration in these Russian fairy tales as well as in the writing of Alexander S. Pushkin. Her beautiful Tatiana Larina doll depicts the heroine in Pushkin's "Eugene Onegin." In this romantic, nineteenth-century poem, Titiana is described as a woman who "loved Russian winters with great passion," including the sleigh rides and the rosy glow of the sunshine on the snow. True to the period of the poem, Stacia's doll wears a Western-influenced costume reminiscent of the 1800s, with strong Victorian overtones.

OPPOSITE, FAR LEFT: **Stacia, Neva Dolls**, Snow Girl, 29 inches, porcelain head, hands and feet, compressed-fabric body, limited to an edition of 5

PHOTO: ALAN BROOKER PHOTOGRAPHY

OPPOSITE PAGE, LEFT: **Stacia, Neva Dolls**, Tatiana Larina, 28 inches, porcelain head, hands and feet, compressed-fabric body, limited to an edition of 20

PHOTO: ALAN BROOKER PHOTOGRAPHY

Helen Kish, Paradise Galleries, Winter, 16 inches, all vinyl, limited to an American edition of 2,500

ABOVE: **Tonner Doll Company,** Ann Estelle by Mary Englebreit 'Queen of Christmas', 8 inches, limited to an edition of 1,000

ABOVE RIGHT: **Alexander Doll Company,** Twelve Days of Christmas, 8 inches, all hard plastic, open edition (comes with a tree containing 12 ornaments)

RIGHT: **Alexander Doll Company,** Waiting for Santa Boy and Waiting for Santa Girl, 8 inches, all hard plastic, open edition

LEFT: **Alexander Doll Company,** Peppermint Swirl, **8 inches, all hard plastic, open edition (issued with the bear)**

BELOW LEFT: **The Vogue Doll Company,** Ginny Snowman, **8 inches, all hard plastic, limited to one year of production**

BELOW: **The Vogue Doll Company,** Ginny's Rockin' Christmas, **8 inches, all hard plastic, limited to an edition of 2,000**

with a bear. The famous New York City company's Twelve Days of Christmas (shown on page 56) has its own miniature Christmas tree, while some of its other holiday dolls carry ornaments made just for them by well-known china companies.

Margie Herrera's Helen—A Scottish Lass (shown on page 53) carries a miniature lantern to light the way on Christmas Even. This doll, says the Wisconsin artist, "was inspired by my Scottish lass mom and her beautiful photos of Scotland in the wintertime." The porcelain doll is a portrait of Herrera's mother when she was young.

Stuffed animals and miniature dollies are also popular accessories for Christmas dolls. Flo Hanover's Brandon (shown on page 49), for example, has a tiny teddy that he's ready to take for a ride on his new sled. (The handmade sled was a gift to the artist from a friend who suggested she use it for a doll – providing the inspiration for this charming little fellow.) Virginia Turner's Zoe (shown on page 64) has her own teddy bear, too, while Seymour Mann's A Christmas Stocking (shown on page 50) holds a little doll.

Italian artist Adriana Rovina Innaciotti has given her red-headed Christmas (shown on page 53) her very own doll, too, perhaps because she knows the pain of not finding a coveted doll

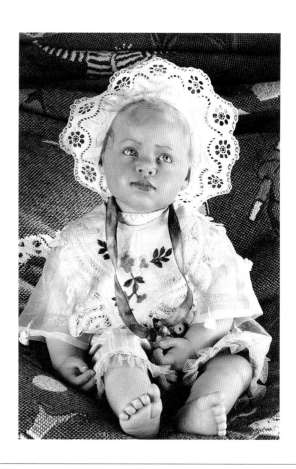

ABOVE, FROM LEFT:
Rotraut Schrott, Little Star, **24 inches, Cernit head and limbs, cloth body, one-of-a-kind**

Sissel Bjorstad Skille, Oda, **26 1/2 inches, Cernit head and limbs, cloth body, one-of-a-kind**

Sissel Bjorstad Skille, Elisabeth, **29 inches, Modelene head and limbs, cloth body, one-of-a-kind**

RIGHT: **Judi L. Thompson,** Snow Children, **3 1/2 to 4 inches, Super Sculpey heads, fabric and wire bodies and limbs, one-of-a-kinds**

SIMPLE JOYS OF AN ITALIAN CHRISTMAS

Lori Falconi spent her childhood in Italy, so Christmas memories take her back to that land where, she says, the holiday was very much a celebration for the birth of Christ. "My cousins and I would await His birth with great anticipation, while enjoying the simplest pleasures the season had to offer." Today, it is the "sights, sounds and tastes of Christmas in Italy that are still very vivid in my mind," she says.

"We lived in a small coastal town. During December, we loved to follow the *Zampognari* through our neighborhood. *Zampognari* are bagpipe musicians, dressed as peasants—in an Italian manger scene, there is usually a figure depicting this character. We would listen to the beautiful music they created with their bagpipes, and as we followed them, we would catch the smell of roasting chestnuts from a corner vendor and wish we had a few.

"Another fond memory is of sitting around the kitchen table, being together with family and friends, eating *panettone* (yeast cakes with raisins) and *torrone* (almond nougat), laughing and telling stories—simple things.

"In my quiet creative moments, when I am working on a Christmas doll," Falconi adds, "those memories are invoked in me. I try to capture this in the simplicity of the dolls I make, and also in the loving attention I give to every detail. I try to create something that will help others step back in time and recall their own happy times."

Helen Kish, Kish & Company, North Pole Riley, 8 inches, all vinyl, limited to an edition of 500

under the Christmas tree. As she explains, "When I was ten years old, I enjoyed playing games with my two brothers—games that at times may have been a bit too agitated. I can only think that I must have been too rambunctious that year, for when Christmas came, I discovered that Santa had brought me absolutely nothing! How many tears I shed. I must have learned my lesson, though, for some days later, to my great surprise, I received a wonderful doll. You can imagine my happiness then, and still today. I love this doll greatly and keep it with me.

"After years devoted to art—to painting and sculpting—I'm now creating artistic dolls, one-of-a-kinds, not intended as toys, but closer to the true reproduction of real children. I try to portray them in usual and common situations, as I meet them in everyday life, and in particular in the unique moments of the Christmas holidays, with all the warm feelings related to these holy days," Innaciotti adds.

English artist Angela Barker, who creates exquisite dolls with her husband, John, says, "Christmas was dolls for me." She had every expectation that she would get just what she wanted—whether she were naughty or nice—for her holiday celebrations began, she explains, "when the mail-order catalog arrived. First, the all-important smell of the catalog itself, then the exquisite pleasure of choosing the Christmas doll. I could have only one, and there were so many to choose from. It was agony; every day I would find the catalog's toy section, go straight to the dolls, and the process would begin all over again. I would go to my mother and ask, 'How big is twenty-four inches?' Always impressed by size, my constant question would be 'which doll is the biggest?'

"The year I was six, the choice was between the most unusual soft fabric doll and a walking-talking doll with an open mouth with teeth, open/close eyes and lovely plaits. I can feel myself making the same choice again, after all these years!

"Now my husband John is my mail-order catalog," she adds, with a smile. "He makes for me beautifully jointed dolls in all sizes, my absolute most favorite being the forty-one-inch lady dolls." Perhaps the greatest pleasure of receiving these dolls from her husband is that she can then delve into her collection of fabulous fabrics and trims and create period costumes that are perfect for their uniquely poseable bodies. That's just what she did with Sophie and Georgina, a delightful twosome who show off their rich Christmas outfits on page 47.

Judi L. Thompson found inspiration for her holiday designs when remembering the "little dolls that hung on the Christmas trees of my childhood." Thompson's Snow Children (shown on page 58), are reminiscent of the German bisque snow babies, or sugar dolls, of the 1890s. These figures, ranging from about two to four inches in height, depicted toddlers in fuzzy white snowsuits, sometimes with red or blue accessories, such as hats, scarves, belts or tights.

There are two theories about the origins of these little holiday figurines. The most appealing is that they were made to commemo-

TOP: Engel-Puppen GmbH, Nikola, 18 inches, vinyl head and limbs, cloth body, limited to an edition of 50 (created exclusively for Disneyland)

ABOVE: Engel-Puppen GmbH, Christina, 20 inches, vinyl head and limbs, cloth body, limited to an edition of 30 (created exclusively for Walt Disney World)

ABOVE: **Anne Myatt**, White Christmas, 15 inches, cloth over Sculpey head, cloth body and limbs with wire armatures, one-of-a-kind

ABOVE RIGHT: **Gaby Rademann**, Hanni, 24 inches, porcelain head and limbs, cloth body, one-of-a-kind

LET'S PARTY!

Doll artist Helen Kish remembers one wild and wonderful Christmas when she was just five years old. "I threw myself a party," she says, "and opened every gift under the tree." It started out innocently enough; she planned to open just one present. She sat down on the floor, picked a gift with her name on it, and began tearing away the paper. Then she noticed her reflection on the blank screen of the family's black-and-white television set. As only a creative child would do, she began acting for the screen, holding up her gift and doing a little advertisement for it. That was fun, so she opened another gift to advertise, and another, and another. By the time her parents found her, all the gifts were open and she was surrounded by mounds and mounds of wrapping paper, boxes and bows. Needless to say, her parents were not pleased.

Kish figures she made up for that naughty Christmas by being very nice on the Christmas Eve of her twelfth year. "My mother went into labor with her eighth child on that Christmas Eve. With both of my parents at the hospital, it was left to the oldest daughter to make Christmas for the little brothers and sister. My mother told me where the presents were hidden and instructed how long to wait before arranging them under the tree. When I was sure that all of my siblings were asleep, my duty as stand-in for Santa began. I remember feeling quite grown-up that night, but it was also bittersweet," she says.

ABOVE LEFT: **Ronna Morse,** Time to Decorate, 16 inches, Super Sculpey head, cloth and wire body and limbs, one-of-a-kind

ABOVE: **Lori Falconi,** Marua and Andrea (with antique baby doll), 28 and 26 inches respectively, all procelain, one-of-a-kind

LEFT: **Katja Schneider,** Oliver, Susi, Tina and Ursel, 20–22 inches, Modelene heads and limbs, cloth bodies, each one-of-a-kind

ABOVE: **Käthe Kruse Puppen GmbH/Europlay Corp.,** Annibelle, 14 inches, composition head, stockinette over sculpted foam body and limbs, limited to an edition of 50

BELOW: **Wendy Lawton, The Lawton Doll Company,** Lilla Brita, 9 inches, porcelain head and hands, wooden body and limbs, limited to an edition of 175

BELOW RIGHT: **Virginia Turner, Turner Dolls, Inc.,** Zoe, silicone-vinyl-blend head and limbs, cloth body, limited to an edition of 100

rate the September 12, 1893, birth of Maria Ahnighito Peary—the daughter of Admiral Robert Edwin Peary and his wife, Josephine. The baby was born in Greenland, where Peary had left his wife while he went off to explore the North Pole.

The Eskimos in Greenland were enamored of the Peary baby and called her Ah-Poo-Mickaninny (which means "snow baby"). Some believe she was given this name because her skin was so very white, compared to the Eskimos' pigmentation; others believe it was for the fleecy white snowsuits that Josephine Peary had made for her baby to protect her from Greenland's bitter cold winters.

The other, less romantic, theory is that the snow baby figures were an outgrowth of *tannenbaumkonfekt*, German sugar dolls first made in the early 1800s out of gum, flour and sugar. Whatever their inspiration, bisque snow baby figurines were produced in Germany from the 1890s until World War II. Among the companies that made them were Bähr & Pröschild; Hertwig & Company and Kley & Hahn. In the 1930s, and again in the 1950s, similar figures were made in Japan. Then, in the mid 1980s, Department 56—an American company well known for its home décor items begun issuing figurines, ornaments and musicals pieces inspired by the early German designs. Department 56 called its designs "Snowbabies."

So many memories inspire today's artists and designers that it is not surprising such a variety of adorable dolls grace the season. Dressed in their holiday best, bundled up and ready to go out and frolic in the snow, or in their pajamas waiting for Santa, these Christmas Kids remind us of carefree times, simple pleasures and the sweet innocence of youth.

Helen Kish, Kish
& Company, Little
Match Girl, 12 1/2
inches, all vinyl,
limited to an
edition of 950

CHAPTER FIVE

Carolers

On this day earth shall ring, With the song children sing
To the Lord, Christ our King, Born on earth to save us.

Maria Saracino, A Dickens Caroling Family,
26 inches, Creall-Therm heads, fabric and
wire limbs, wood, wire and fabric bodies,
one-of-a-kinds

THE SONGS OF THE CHRISTMAS SEASON ARE SURELY SOME OF the most beautiful, most melodic ever written. But Christmas wasn't always celebrated with carols, although music or chanting has regularly been a part of Christian worship. Indeed, music predates recorded history and, say some scholars, may predate human speech. Archeologists have found musical instruments dating back approximately 30,000 years, and folk music and group singing was common in many early civilizations.

The tradition of Western choral music has its roots in the Jewish and Greek cultures. The Old Testament contains numerous references to singing, as well as to choral music, and there were synagogue choirs throughout ancient Israel. The drama of ancient Greece is distinguished by its chorus, which grew out of the singing and dancing of pagan religious festivals. In fact, the root of the word "chorus" is from the Greek word *choros*, which means circle dance. (The English word "carol" stems from the Greek *chor-aulos*: a combination of two words, *choros* and *aulos*, the name of a reed instrument.)

Among the early Christians were synagogue cantors, who are credited with bringing a rich musical tradition to what was then a new religious movement. By the second century, hymns were being sung by choirs as part of worship services, most particularly in Eastern churches. After Christianity was sanctioned by the Roman emperor Constantine the Great in 313, Pope Sylvester I founded a choir school in Rome. Since then, sacred music has been a part of Christian worship around the world.

Carols, which are defined as songs of rejoicing, have their roots in folk music, and are distinguished by melodies that are lighter and gayer than hymns. They were included in the midnight service that

St. Francis of Assisi held in a cave in Greccio in 1223, when he first created a nativity scene to commemorate the birth of Christ. Over the next century, carols became a part of Christmas celebrations throughout Europe.

Caroling—the public singing of carols— is believed to have begun in the 1400s, when wandering minstrels performed songs in exchange for donations to the needy. This early caroling was not limited to Christmas, although it was associated with religious holidays. Later, English waits (night watchmen) began to sing carols at Christmastime as they patrolled the streets. Most, but not all, of the

Byers' Choice Ltd., Carolers, adults: 13 inches, children: 9 inches; clay heads, poured plaster bases, bodies, arms and legs, tissue paper sculpted around wire armatures, handcrafted, so no two are alike

Xenis Collection Ltd., Nicholas and Noelle, 15 inches, all wood, limited to an edition of 40 (have 18-note musicals inside; boy plays *Deck the Halls*, girl plays *Winter Wonderland*)

Marilyn Henke, Hark, It's Harold, 18 inches, polymer-clay head and limbs, cloth-over-wire body, one-of-a-kind

songs they sang referred to the Virgin Mary and Christ's birth. While many of the earliest carols have been lost, there are printed records of carols dating back to the 1500s.

With the Protestant Reformation and the establishment of the Lutheran Church, congregational singing became part of worship services. (Prior to this, sacred music was performed in services by choirs.) This, in turn, promoted the composition of new music, including a variety of Christmas carols. The Reverend Martin Luther is credited with writing the verses for several Christmas carols that remain popular today; they include "From Heaven Above to Earth I Come" and the better known "Away in A Manger."

Christmas carols became so popular by the mid-seventeenth century that when the celebration of Christmas was banned in many places, carols continued to be sung by people in their homes. Christmas caroling became popular in Victorian England, and in nineteenth-century America, due in part to the writings of Charles Dickens and Washington Irving. In *The Sketchbook of Geoffrey Crayon, Gent.*, for instance, Irving writes about awakening from a deep sleep to hear the waits singing, and "connecting them with the sacred and joyous occasion, have almost fancied them into another celestial choir, announcing peace and good-will to mankind."

The joys of caroling—singing with others or being visited by a group of carolers—is one of the great delights of the Christmas season. It is not surprising, then, that some of our Christmas dolls depict these holiday singers.

Joyce Patterson's God Rest You Merry Gentlemen (shown on page 70 and named for the title of an old English carol) was inspired by "memories from the early years (1970s) of Galveston's Dickens on the Strand Celebration," says the Texas dollmaker. "I patterned their clothing after nineteenth-century Dickens' characters," she adds. The tableau was also influenced by early magazine-cover art by the great American illustrator Norman Rockwell.

Many of the carolers from Byers' Choice also have a Dickensian appearance, but the Tonner Doll Company's little caroler is a thoroughly modern miss. "One of my most favorite traditions during Christmas is an old-fashioned caroling," says artist Robert Tonner. "Nothing seems to mark the season quite like the sound of familiar Christmas songs, and I'm always delighted to hear our neighborhood children sing them." Thus, he says, "in reviewing Mary Engelbreit's artwork, I was charmed by her little caroling girl—she seemed to epitomize the quintessential caroler.

"Mary never makes my job easy," adds Tonner, who has created dolls based on a number of Engelbreit's whimsical illustrations. "She draws whatever comes into her head, and it's up to me—and my designer, Joe Petrollese—to interpret her designs. We are determined to get them right! I love the way this little caroler turned out—I think she is very true to the original sketch."

The designers at Xenis Collection are, like Robert Tonner, fans of caroling. "On a cold December evening it is magical to hear the ringing of bells and the faint murmur of caroling," they say. "This is the only time when we freely invite strangers into our homes to share cookies and hot cocoa. We wanted to bring this magic to life and make it last year-round with a pair of musical carolers. Nicholas and Noelle (shown on opposite page) are here to remind us that Christmas has always been, and should still be, about making and sharing memories."

Tonner Doll Company, Sophie by Mary Engelbreit, Caroling Girl, 10 inches, all vinyl, limited to an edition of 1,000 (comes with resin caroling book)

ABOVE: **Joyce Patterson,** God Rest You Merry Gentlemen, **10 to 17 inches, all cloth, one-of-a-kind tableau**

OPPOSITE PAGE: **Byers' Choice Ltd.,** Carolers, **adults: 13 inches, children: 9 inches; clay heads, poured-plaster bases, bodies, arms and legs, tissue paper sculpted around wire armatures, hand-crafted, so no two are alike**

DID YOU KNOW?

One of the world's favorite carols exists because of a broken-down church organ. Josef Mohr, the Vicar of St. Nicholas Church in Obendorf, was upset because the church's old organ was, once again, not working. The year was 1818, and twenty-six-year-old Mohr couldn't imagine a Christmas Eve service without music. So he asked his friend Franz X. Gruber—a schoolteacher and the church's organist—to compose music for a poem that Mohr had written a few years earlier, and to perform it, accompanied by his guitar, at the Christmas Eve service. Gruber agreed, and on December 24, 1818, "Silent Night, Holy Night" debuted.

This wonderful Christmas carol may well have been lost were it not for Carl Mauracher. In 1825, when he was commissioned to repair the Obendorf church's organ, Mauracher found a handwritten copy of it in the church, complete with musical notations. A resident of the Tyrol region, known for its choral groups, he took the music home with him. Soon it was being performed throughout the region.

In 1854, the director of the Royal Court Choir in Berlin traced the carol's origins. Final proof of the Mohr-Gruber collaboration was discovered many years later when an 1820 manuscript by Josef Mohr was found in Salzburg; in it, Mohn credits the "melodie" to "Fr. Xav. Gruber."

Holiday Classics

Oh, there's no place like home for the holidays, 'Cause no matter how far away you roam...

Betty Coven, *Sugar Plum Fairy*, 18 inches, ProSculpt head and limbs, fabric-over-wire body, one-of-a-kind

S O MUCH OF THE HAPPINESS OF THE CHRISTMAS SEASON comes from remembering and observing traditions. For many of us, holiday traditions include attending a performance of *A Christmas Carol* or *The Nutcracker* ballet. These Christmas classics—both based on books written more than a century and a half ago—are enjoyed by millions over and over again. Both also have inspired numerous works of art, including some outstanding dolls.

In 1843, when Charles Dickens (1812-1870) wrote *A Christmas Carol*, life was bleak for the lower classes. The Industrial Revolution had brought many farm laborers to the cities, where work hours were long and pay was low. The poor lived in squalor, child labor was common and people were imprisoned for debt. There was little time to celebrate Christmas, but the publication of *A Christmas Carol* began to change the way that people thought about the holiday.

When Charles Dickens was twelve years old, his father was thrown into debtor's prison and young Charles went to work in a factory to help support his family. Later he returned to his studies, worked as a law office clerk, a shorthand reporter, and then as an essayist and fiction writer. He spent much of his life campaigning against social injustice, a subject woven through many of his novels.

OPPOSITE PAGE: **Paradise Galleries commissioned doll artist Patricia Rose to create this set of five resin ornaments based on the graceful dancers of Tchiakovsky's beloved Nutcracker Suite. The set features the Sugar Plum Fairy in soft pink and with outstretched wings; Winged Dewdrop on pointe and wearing a yellow tutu; and Snowflake, shimmering in ice blue. Completing the set is Clara and the handsome Nutcracker Prince.**

TOP: **Maria Saracino,** God Bless Us Everyone,
24 inches, all Pro-Sculpt, one-of-a-kind

ABOVE: **Maria Saracino,** Scrooge with the
Ghost of Christmas Past, 22 inches, Creall-
Therm head, wire and fabric limbs, wood,
wire and fabric body, one-of-a-kind

In the preface to A *Christmas Carol,* Dickens writes: "I have endeavoured in this Ghostly little book to raise the Ghost of an Idea which shall not put my readers out of humour with themselves, with each other, with the season, or with me. May it haunt their house pleasantly, and no one wish to lay it." And so it did, and so it does.

As all who make A *Christmas Carol* a part of their holidays know, it is the story of a miser, Ebenezer Scrooge, who scorns his only relative, his nephew Fred Fezziwig, a pleasant young fellow who always invites Scrooge to share Christmas dinner at his home, and is mean to his kind clerk, Bob Cratchit, who doesn't let his dreary work days ruin his happy home life. And he never gives to charity. All in all, Scrooge is a miserable old curmudgeon, whose only delight is in being shunned by those around him.

One Christmas Eve, seven years after the death of his partner, Jacob Marley, Scrooge is visited by Marley's Ghost, who has a chain "wound about him like a tail." Marley, who was as avaricious as Scrooge, warns him that it is required of everyone "that the spirit within him should walk abroad among his fellow-men, and travel far and wide; and if that spirit goes not forth in life, it is condemned to do so after death." Thus, Marley's Ghost says, since his death he has been traveling the world seeing what he might have shared on earth and turned to happiness. Marley warns that Scrooge will share his fate after death if he doesn't change his ways. To help him see the light, Marley tells Scrooge, he will be haunted by three spirits.

Scrooge is then visited by the Ghost of Christmas Past, which takes him back to happy times in his childhood and reminds him of the love of his deceased sister, the mother of his well-wishing nephew Fred. The Ghost of Christmas Present then takes him to (invisibly) visit the meager but happy Christmas celebrations of the Cratchits, where he learns that the youngest, Tiny Tim, suffers from a crippling disease, as well as to a Christmas party at the Fezziwigs, where he discovers how others perceive his lonely, stingy life. Lastly, he is shown how poor people around the world find and share joy in the holiday season.

The final visitor, the Ghost of Christmas Future, shows Scrooge

CHRISTMAS TRIVIA

Don't worry about the Grinch, or the bah humbugs of Scrooge. The people who did the most to steal Christmas in America were the Puritans. According to the Hoover Library's *The Legends of Christmas,* back in 1659 the Puritan powers-that-be decided that people were using the holiday as an excuse to drink too much and overeat, so they made celebrating Christmas illegal. For almost two hundred years, Christmas was pretty much ignored in the United States. Indeed, as late as the 1870s, children attended school on Christmas Day, and adults went to work.

Byers' Choice Ltd, from left: Mrs. Cratchit, Spirit of Christmas Future, Bob Cratchit & Tiny Tim, Scrooge, Spirit of Christmas Present and Marley's Ghost, 13 inches, clay heads, poured-plaster bases, bodies, arms and legs, tissue paper sculpted around wire armatures, 2004 A Christmas Carol series

not only his own death—mourned by none and followed by tradespeople picking over his belongings—but also the death of Tiny Tim, who is lovingly remembered by his family. The visitation of these ghosts has a profound effect on Scrooge, who promises the Ghost of Christmas Future that he will "honor Christmas in his heart, and try to keep it all the year," if he can change the future.

A changed man when he wakes on Christmas morning, Scrooge immediately takes steps to alter his miserly ways and proceeds to live an exemplary life, helping others, finding happiness in his heart and keeping Christmas well.

Is it any wonder that for more than 160 years, Dickens' tale and its ghosts have continued to haunt the holidays in such winning ways? What a wonderful reminder that Christmas is not what we get at the

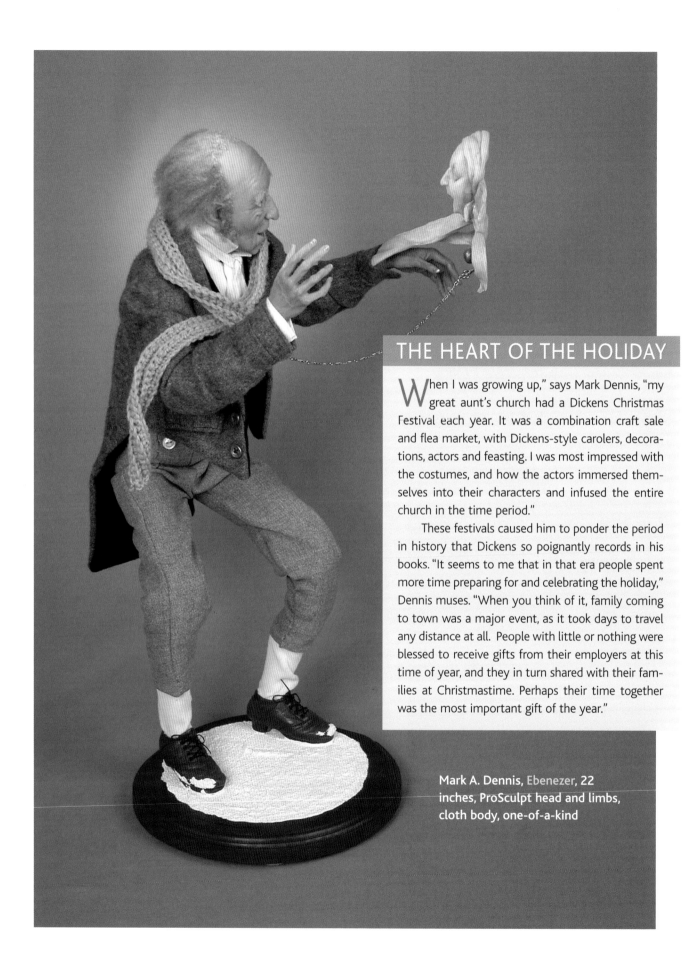

THE HEART OF THE HOLIDAY

W hen I was growing up," says Mark Dennis, "my great aunt's church had a Dickens Christmas Festival each year. It was a combination craft sale and flea market, with Dickens-style carolers, decorations, actors and feasting. I was most impressed with the costumes, and how the actors immersed themselves into their characters and infused the entire church in the time period."

These festivals caused him to ponder the period in history that Dickens so poignantly records in his books. "It seems to me that in that era people spent more time preparing for and celebrating the holiday," Dennis muses. "When you think of it, family coming to town was a major event, as it took days to travel any distance at all. People with little or nothing were blessed to receive gifts from their employers at this time of year, and they in turn shared with their families at Christmastime. Perhaps their time together was the most important gift of the year."

Mark A. Dennis, Ebenezer, 22 inches, ProSculpt head and limbs, cloth body, one-of-a-kind

holidays or, indeed, what we get in life itself, but rather, what we give.

"So memorable are the characters in this tale," says Pennsylvania artist Mark Dennis, "that a few suggestions of costume and the proper setting, and anyone can recognize Scrooge or Tiny Tim. They are ingrained in our culture, which makes them easy to present as art dolls. All you need to do is present the image and the viewer fills in the story, with all their feelings from years of recognition."

Among the artist's recent pieces based on *A Christmas Carol* is Scrooge, whom Dennis has portrayed "at his counting table, counting out his coins and balancing the day's books. He looks up with his icy stare as this most important work has been interrupted." In another piece, Ebenezer, Dennis depicts Scrooge when he first glimpses Marley's Ghost as he puts his key into the keyhole of his front door.

Maria Saracino has also found inspiration in Dickens' ghosts. Her Scrooge with the Ghost of Christmas Past (shown on page 74) presents a grumpy old man about to encounter the first of the three Christmas ghosts. Other dolls based on Dickens' "Ghostly little book," depict Bob Cratchit and Tiny Tim, and the story's happy ending.

Like the plays and movies based on *A Christmas Carol*, *The Nutcracker* ballet is based on a book: *The Nutcracker and the Mouse King*, by Ernst Theodor Amadeus Hoffman (1776-1822). Hoffman was born in Koningsberg, Germany. Something of a Renaissance man, he wrote operas, a symphony and various choral and piano works, and worked as an orchestra conductor and a critic. Hoffman wrote *The Nutcracker and the Mouse King* in 1816, when he was working in the Supreme Court of Berlin. *The Nutcracker* ballet, which has made this story famous, is considered a children's tale. Hoffman's original, however, is considered a story about children at Christmastime, rather than

Mark A. Dennis, Scrooge, 16 inches, ProSculpt head and limbs, cloth-over-wire body, one-of-a-kind

Tonner Doll Company, Nutcracker
Prince, Sugar Plum Fairy, and Clara,
14 and 19 inches, all porcelain,
limited to editions of 200 each

one for children. In fact, *The Nutcracker* ballet is actually based on a
softened version of Hoffman's story, a translation by French author
Alexandre Dumas.

The first presentation of this ballet was choreographed by
Marius Petipa—a French choreographer considered the creator of
modern classical ballet, who commissioned Russian composer Pyotr
Illich Tchaikovsky to write the music for *The Nutcracker* ballet. It
was performed at the Mariinsky Theater, home of Russia's famed
Kirov Ballet.

The story begins at a Christmas party at the Stahlbaums' home,
where the hosts' son and daughter, Fritz and Clara, are present. All is
festive when the children's godfather Drosselmeyer arrives with gifts
for Fritz and Clara. Clara receives a nutcracker, which Fritz wishes
were his. In a fit of jealousy, he breaks it. Their godfather, a clock
and toy maker, repairs it with what appears to be a magic handker-

Patricia Rose, Paradise Galleries, Sugar Plum Fairy, 14 inches, porcelain head and limbs, cloth body, limited to an edition of 100,000

ABOVE: **Byers' Choice Ltd.**, from left: Marie, Louis Playing the Piano and Fritz, **9 inches**, clay heads, poured-plaster bases, bodies, arms and legs, tissue paper sculpted around wire armatures, open editions

OPPOSITE PAGE, ABOVE RIGHT: **Flo Hanover**, Clara, **14½ inches seated**, Cernit head and limbs, cloth body with wire armature, one-of-a-kind

OPPOSITE PAGE, RIGHT: **Flo Hanover**, Clara, **15 inches seated**, Cernit head and limbs, cloth body with wire armature, one-of-a-kind

chief and gives it back to Clara, who falls asleep behind the Christmas tree with the nutcracker nestled at her side.

Now comes the crux of the ballet: Clara's dream. As the clock strikes midnight, she shrinks to the size of her toys, which all come alive, along with an army of mice led by a seven-headed Mouse King. Clara's nutcracker gathers an army of toy soldiers and they battle the mice. As the nutcracker's battle is all but lost, Clara saves the day by throwing her slipper at the Mouse King and knocking him out. The mice retreat, and the nutcracker turns into a prince and takes Clara first to the Land of Snow, then to the Land of Sweets. They tell of their battle with the mice and the Sugar Plum Fairy rewards them with a series of dances. In some versions, the ballet ends with Clara and the Prince riding an airborne sleigh into the

FROM FAIRY TO BALLERINA

A longtime fan of *The Nutcracker* ballet, Boxborough, Massachusetts, artist Flo Hanover has created several dolls based on it, including Clara and Sugar Plum Fairy. But her Trina as a Sugar Plum Fairy had different roots. "I admired the fairy dolls my friends made, so decided to try making one myself. But for some reason, my fairy looked like a little girl pretending to be a fairy," Hanover admits. "She reminded me of the children that dance in Nutcracker productions, so that's what I decided to make her. Her outfit is made of pink taffeta topped by a sheer embroidered fabric, and her wings are a combination of paper, lace and feathers."

Flo Hanover, *Trina as a Sugar Plum Fairy*, 13 inches seated, Cernit head and limbs, cloth body with wire armature, one-of-a-kind

winter skies. In others, Clara awakes to find herself still behind the tree with the nutcracker lovingly clasped in her arms.

Over the years, thousands of children around the world have performed in *The Nutcracker* ballet. Some dance companies perform the original Petipa choreography; others have re-staged this Christmas classic, which was first performed in America in 1940 by the Ballet Russe. In 1944 William Christensen choreographed the first full-length American version for the San Francisco Ballet. In 1954, George Balanchine choreographed *The Nutcracker* for the New York City Ballet. The company, including two alternate casts of children from the company's School of American Ballet, has performed it annually ever since. The production features elaborate costumes, including a nine-foot-wide, eighty-five-pound outfit for Mother Ginger, an on-stage snowstorm and a one-ton Christmas tree that grows on stage to a height of forty feet.

Great music, great dance, fantastic settings and a story with a happy ending: *The Nutcracker* ballet may not have the sentiment of *A Christmas Carol*, but it's no less appealing to children and adults, including some of today's splendid dollmakers.

Gloria Tepper, Sugar Plum from Nutcracker Suite, **17 inches, stoneware clay head and limbs, cloth body, one-of-a-kind**

DID YOU KNOW?

The fir tree is believed to have been a symbol of Christianity since circa 1000. According to legend, Saint Boniface (who is credited with converting Germans to Christianity) was strolling through the woods one day when he ran into some pagans worshipping an oak tree. He must have been furious, for he chopped down the mighty oak. When a fir tree sprang up from the oak tree's roots, Boniface took this as a sign from God and thus the fir tree became a symbol of the Christian faith.

The German tradition of bringing fir trees inside and decorating them for Christmas dates from the 1500s. German immigrants to the United States brought the custom of trimming a tree with them in the 1700s. England's Queen Victoria introduced the custom to her country in 1848; no doubt to please her German husband, Prince Albert, she included a Christmas tree as part of the holiday decorations that year at Windsor Castle. Slowly, the custom spread through much of the world.

According to University of Illinois research, Christmas trees have been sold commercially in the United States for about 150 years. Some 35 million Christmas trees are produced here annually. If you think that's a lot of trees, consider this: About half the Christmas trees in American homes today are artificial.

Now here's happy news: The Christmas tree industry is good for your health, as well as for the American economy. One acre of Christmas trees supplies the daily oxygen needs of eighteen people. In 2002, more than 445,000 acres of land were planted in Christmas trees, supplying not only a heck of a lot of oxygen, but also providing employment for some 100,000 people.

First family fir facts: In 1856, Franklin Pierce became the first President to place a Christmas tree in the White House. President Calvin Coolidge started the national Christmas Tree Lighting Ceremony on the White House lawn in 1923. Teddy Roosevelt banned Christmas trees from the White House during his presidency for environmental reasons. In 1963, the National Christmas Tree remained dark until December 22, because of the thirty-day period of mourning for President John F. Kennedy. In 1979—in honor of the American hostages in Iran—only the top ornament on the National Christmas Tree was lit.

Wendy Lawton, The
Lawton Doll Company,
Nutcracker, 14 inches,
all porcelain, limited
edition of 500

Chapter Seven

Christmas Wrappings

Deck the halls with boughs of holly...'Tis the season to be jolly...
Don we now our gay apparel.

THESE FASHIONABLE DOLLS ARE ALL WRAPPED UP IN THEIR
holiday finery, reminding us that Christmas is a festive time, full of
parties with family and friends. The holiday season culminates on
New Year's Eve and what, for many, is the greatest party of the winter as it marks the end of one year and the beginning of an exciting
new one.

Whether sweet or sassy, these fashionable dolls know that it's not
easy to compete with the profuse decorations of the holidays, but
they're surely willing to try—and who would doubt that they'll suc-
ceed? As you can see, they've decked themselves out in the colors of
the season to rival the most lavishly wrapped gifts, sparkling ornaments and beautifully decorated Christmas trees. Some of their outfits rival the richness of the robes worn by the Wise Men from the
East, while others have the simple shimmer of a star or ice crystal.

While we (and our dolls) enjoy donning our gay apparel, imagine the joy of creating such luscious looks for a delectable fashion
doll's body. Robert Tonner—who began his career as a fashion
designer of women's apparel and now heads the Tonner Doll
Company—gets to do just that. "Designing for Tyler and Sydney is
always fun and a challenge," Tonner says, "but never more so than
at the holidays. I try to remain true to Tyler's high-fashion roots; I
want to invoke the season, but at the same time, her style needs to
be high fashion and sophisticated. I always start with color—and
Christmas colors are easy to determine—but red seems to always be
at the top of the list. A beautiful red, a little sparkle, a great shape

**Xenis Collection Ltd., Lauryn, 23 inches, all wood (western maple),
limited to an edition of 75**

Mattel, Winter Fantasy
Barbie, 11½ inches, all
vinyl, Collector Edition
2003/closed

Juanita F. Montoya, Ruby,
43 inches, poured-wax
head, wax limbs, fabric
body with armature,
one-of-a-kind

Mattel, Holiday Celebration Barbie, 11 ½ inches, all vinyl, Special Edition 2001/closed

Donna RuBert, Paradise Galleries, Ashley Belle, 22 inches, porcelain head and limbs, cloth body, limited to an edition of 100,000

PERIOD PERFECT FOR PRESENTS

From her towering hairdo to the bottom of her skirt, Elizabeth Jenkins' Winter Wish Princess would be right at home at a holiday party in the late 1500s. Women's fashions were fabulous back then, but far from comfortable to wear. Dresses featured bodices that extended down into a V, accentuating a woman's tightly corseted waist, and skirts that jutted stiffly out from the hips and were padded with swirls of fabric, and then richly adorned.

The inspiration for this doll stems from the artist's childhood. "When I was a little girl, our town museum sponsored a Winter Fairy Princess as a holiday event for children, rather than featuring the ubiquitous Santa," she says. "Usually, a teenage beauty queen would add a 'magic wand' to her prom dress and crown. But in my imagination, she looked like this figure: glamorous, yet infinitely gracious and motherly. White cotton-candy hair, clothes made of drifts of snow ice cream and mounds of snowballs, in a style of a far-more-romantic time long ago. Her rosy cheeks and eyelashes would constantly glitter with the diamond sparkles of tiny snowdrops."

Elizabeth Jenkins, Winter Wish Princess, 32 inches, Paperclay head and arms, wire and batting body, one-of-a-kind

DID YOU KNOW?

No one quite knows the origins of wreaths. The accepted theory is that they stem from ancient Greece, when diadems (from the Greek word *diadema*, meaning "thing bound round") were popular head adornments. Beginning in 776 B.C., the winners of the various Olympic games were awarded diadems made of laurel leaves. It is assumed that, proud of their accomplishments, they hung these circlets of laurel on their doors to let others know of their victories—thus starting the custom of wreaths as outdoor decorations. The Romans decorated their heads with diadems, too; they also used them to honor athletes and valorous soldiers. Roman diadems grew more elaborate over time and evolved into crowns made of precious metals and studded with gems.

An alternate theory is that Christmas wreaths stem from Christ's death: that they symbolize his crown of thorns, with the holly berries denoting his blood. Thus the hanging of a wreath to celebrate Christmas commemorates not only the birth of Jesus, but also the everlasting life that his death on the cross made possible. In addition, these circular decorations, which have no beginning and no end, symbolize the eternity of God.

For most people today, a wreath is hung as a sign of welcome. Made of holly and mistletoe, evergreen boughs or grapevine, they are decorated much like Christmas trees; some sport tiny lights, ornaments, fancy ribbons, even teddy bears and dolls. Others are adorned with pine cones and berries.

Advent wreaths are unadorned except for four candles (three violet and one rose, or all four white). Advent wreaths are not hung on doors, but rather are placed on a table or chest, generally with a larger candle inside the ring of greenery. Advent wreaths were first used by Christians in Germany sometime in the fifteenth or sixteenth century. The four candles denote the four weeks of Advent, which begins four Sundays before Christmas. Each week a new candle is lit, denoting a family's preparations for the holidays, until Christmas Eve, when the center candle is lit to commemorate Christ's birth.

Tonner Doll Company, Santa Baby Tyler, 16 inches, vinyl head, vinyl/hard-plastic body and limbs, one-of-a-kind (wearing Santa Baby outfit for her appearance on NBC's "Today Show")

Tonner Doll Company, Tiny Kitty Collier™ Hatbox Gift Set, 10 inches, hard plastic, limited to an edition of 1,500

OPPOSITE PAGE, RIGHT: **Mattel,** Celebration Barbie, **11¹/₂ inches, all vinyl, Special Edition 2000/closed**

FAR RIGHT: **Mattel,** 2004 Holiday Barbie, **11¹/₂ inches, all vinyl, open edition**

BELOW RIGHT: **Alexander Doll Company,** Santa Baby Alexandra Fairchild Ford™, **16 inches, vinyl head, plastic body, open edition**

Mattel, Holiday Celebration Barbie, **11¹/₂ inches, all vinyl, Special Edition 2002/closed**

and Tyler and Sydney are ready for a holiday party!

"Growing up in a small town in Indiana," adds Tonner, "I didn't have a lot of ways to experience the glamour of fashion. But one way I was able to do it was to see the new dolls in the stores at Christmastime. I remember seeing those dolls—the glamour dolls of the 1950s, and the wonderful dolls done by Mattel and Ideal—fill the shelves of the local hardware store (there was no toy store in Bluffton, Indiana!). It was always a magical time for me, and those memories still inspire me to create beautifully dressed dolls for the holidays."

Shown here with Tonner's beauties are some of Mattel's twenty-first-century Holiday Barbies, along with many other lovely ladies from a smattering of individual doll artists and companies. We know that these stylish beauties join with the angels, the Santas, the carolers, the Christmas kids and all the other delightful dolls that mark the holidays to wish you a Merry Christmas and a Happy New Year.

And maybe as the year runs out, you'll hear them softly singing of good times past and still to come as Tiny Tim whispers in his sweet voice, "God bless us, every one."

Tonner Doll Company, from left: Esme, Carrie Chan, an unnamed character, Angelina Ruiz, Tyler Wentworth and Sydney Chase, 16 inches, prototypes (dolls model 2004 Ready-to-Wear Red Holiday Boutique Collection, limited to 500 pieces each)

DIRECTORY OF ARTISTS & MANUFACTURERS

Abaimova, Tanya
127 Wigton Circle
Perkasie, PA 18944
(215) 249-1661
info@sunnyfaces.net
www.sunnyfaces.net

Alexander Doll Company
615 West 131st St.
New York, NY 10027
(212) 283-5900
www.madamealexander.com

Antolick, Terry
35664 Stevens Blvd.
Eastlake, OH 44095
(440) 951-9479
no-tua-lyke@sbc.global.net

Baker, Betsey P.
81 Hy Vue Terrace
Cold Spring, NY 10516
(845) 265-3490
rnbaker@att_global.net

Bansmer, Glenda
6007 Glacier Way
Yakima, WA 98908
(509) 965-4960
GlendaBansmer1@aol.com

Barker, Angela and John
62 Woodside View
Cottingley, Bingley
W. Yorkshire, BD16 1RL
England
011-44-1274-565944
ajceramics@talk21.com

Bolden, Marilyn
2286 Alligator Creek Rd.
Clearwater, FL 33765
(727) 797-5342
MariD2286@aol.com

Byers' Choice Ltd.
PO Box 158
Chalfont, PA 18914
(215) 822-6700
Fax: (215) 822-3847
www.byerschoice.com

Byrnes, Betty Lou
2409 Marshall Ct.

Naperville, IL 60565
(630) 416-1463
dblbyrnes@wideopenwest.com

Casper, Cindy
1855 Fifth St.
Cuyahoga Falls
OH 44221
(330) 923-0685
ccasp@neo.rr.com

Coe, Jan
1229 Edenbridge Way
Knoxville, TN 37923
(865) 481-4708
jancoe@westcotech.com

Coleman-Cobb, Patricia
PO Box 2595
Duluth, GA 30096
(770) 622-2164
Lcobbster@aol.com

Collins, Penny
N3550 Hwy. 12
Mauston, WI 53948
(608) 847-5014
penny@thumbprintartworx.com

Coven, Betty
2761 Renshaw Dr.
Troy, MI 48085
(248) 528-3076
betty@numan.com

Daanen, Ankie
Stadionkade 12 II
1077 VJ Amsterdam
The Netherlands
011-20-679-5300
Fax: 011-20-679-5074
ankiedaanen@hotmail.com

DeHoff, Dave
185 Bankert Rd.
Hanover, PA 17331
www.creativegalleries.com

Dennis, Mark A.
122 Manor Ave.
Millersville, PA 17551
(717) 872-8343
www.mad-sculptor.com

DiPonte, Nancy
4 Kimball Ave.
Johnston, RI 02919
(401) 944-9349
nadiponte@yahoo.com

Effanbee Doll Company
459 Hurley Ave.
Hurley, NY 12443
(845) 339-8246
Fax: (845) 339-8326
www.effanbeedoll.com

Engel-Puppen GmbH
Moenchroedener Str. 55
96472 Roedental, Germany
Markus.Engel@engelpuppen.com

Falconi, Lori
16 Highland Hill
Toronto, Ontario
Canada
(416) 782-2748
Lorellafalconi@hotmail.com

Flaga, Pauline
1033 W. Elmwood blvd.
Clawson, MI 48017
(248) 435-4567
pauline@flaga.net

Hanover, Flo
71 Boxmill Rd.
Boxborough, MA 01719
(978) 263-3250

Henke, Marilyn
5422 SW 43rd Ave.
Owatonna, MN 55060
(507) 451-8979
Mhenke99@HickoryTech.net

Herrera, Margie
688 Lower Kimo Dr.
Kula, HI 96790
(808) 298-1854
c.herrera4@verizon.net

Hume, Pepper
2431 Spring Stuebner
Spring, TX 77389
(281) 795-0936
pepperh@ev1.net

Innaciotti, Adriana Rovina
Via Alighiero, 20
46047 Porto Mantovano (MN)
Italy
011-39-0376-398341
Info@adrianadolls.com

Jenkins, Elizabeth
8203 N.W. Oregon
Kansas City, MO 64151
(816) 587-5871
Jenkart@hotmail.com

Johnston, Jack
Johnston Original Artdolls
530 Tanglewood Loop
North Salt Lake City,
UT 84054
(800) 290-9998
www.artdolls.com

Jones, Bonnie
102 Catalpa Dr.
Natchez. MS 39102
(601) 442-4597
Bonniej@cableone.net

Käthe Kruse Puppen
GmbH/Europlay Corp.
22 Westover Rd.
Troy, NY 12180
(518) 273-0726
Fax: (518) 273-0754
www.kathekruse.com

Kawalez, Marlene
437 Highside Dr.
Milton, Ontario
Canada L9T 1W9
(905) 876-3309
marlenek@cogeco.ca

Kays, Linda J.
42 Mitchell St.
Norwich, NY 13815
(607) 336-2642
www.LindaKays.com

Kertzman, Linda S.
PO Box 98
Morris, NY 13808
(607) 263-5988
www.lindakertzman.com

Kish, Helen
Kish & Company
1800 W 33rd Ave.
Denver, CO 80211
(303) 972-0053

Lawton, Wendy
The Lawton Doll Company
548 North First St.
Turlock, CA 95380
(209) 632-3655
CustomerService@LawtonDolls.com
www.LawtonDolls.com

Lee Middleton Original Dolls
480 Olde Worthington Rd.
Ste.110
Westerville, OH 43082
(614) 797-4639
www.leemiddleton.com

Mason, Linda
(see Paradise Galleries)

Mattel, Inc.
333 Continental Blvd.
El Segundo, CA 90245
(310) 252-2000
www.mattel.com

Montoya, Juanita F.
1437 Blue Jay Circle
Weston, FL 33327
(954) 217-0331
jmdollart@aol.com

Morse, Ronna
42908 Secretariat Ct.
Ashburn, VA 20147
(703) 724-0563
morsedolls@aol.com

Mousa, Margaret
21 Callum St.
Mooroobool, Cairns
Queensland 4870
Australia
001-61-7-4032-3128
mousa@ozemail.com.au
www.mmousadolls.com

Myatt, Anne
6910 Cypress Point Dr.
Houston, TX 77069
(281) 580-8005
justlikemedolls@att.net

Neva Dolls by Stacia
35 Bedminster Terrace
Bedminster, NJ 07921
(908) 470-1930

Fax: (908) 470-1931
www.nevadolls.com

Pannell, Mazie
Annastasia's Dolls
6717 Brants Lane
Fort Worth
TX 76116
(817) 738-7800
www.anastasiasdolls.com

Paradise Galleries
11696 Sorrento Valley Rd., Ste.A
San Diego, CA 92121
(858) 793-4000
www.paradisegalleries.com

Patterson, Joyce
PO Box 1599
Brazoria
TX 77422
(979) 798-9890
clothdol@txbs.net
www.joycepatterson.com

Piper, Carole
73 Fairlawn Dr.
East Grinstead
Sussex RH19 1NS
England
011-13-42-323-373

Rademann, Gaby
Aseuhauer Weg 1A
84564 Oberberg Kirchen
Germany
kar.ade@freenet.de

Roche, Lynne and Michael
2 Lansdown Terrace,
Lansdown Rd. Bath BA1 5EF
England
01225-318042
lynne@roche-dolls.co.uk
www.roche-dolls.co.uk

Romero, Debra Parker
3525 rolling Creek Dr.
Buford, GA 30519
(678) 546-3767
Hobb1@Bellsouth.net

Rose, Patricia
(see Paradise Galleries)

Ross, Trina Neher
Original Artist Dolls
6653 Liebler Rd.
Boston, NY 14025
(716) 941-6512
tnross@aol.com

RuBert, Donna
(see Paradise Galleries &
Seymour Mann, Inc.)

Rush, Candace
31 Longfellow Dr.
Coventry, RI 02816
(401) 828-5186

Saracino, Maria
43 Saginaw Crescent
Nepean, Ontario
K2E 6Y8 Canada
(613) 723-5226
mariasaracino@saracino.ca

Schneider, Katja
Elchstr. 7
41564 Kaarst
Germany
011-21-3160-4060
Katja.Schneider.Kaarst@t-Online.de
www.RKS-Puppen.com

Schrott, Rotraut
Spitzingstrasse 1
85598 Baldham
Germany
011-49-8106-8031

Scully, Barbara
519 Magic Oaks Dr.
Spring, TX 77388
(281) 350-1354
bobbie21@flash.net

Seymour Mann, Inc.
230 Fifth Avenue
New York, NY 10001
(212) 683-7262
Fax: (212) 213-4920

Sherrod, Myra
Born Yesterday Art Dolls, Inc.
1251 Garden Circle Dr., 2C-C
St. Louis, MO 63125
(314) 894-1489
bydolls@charter.net

Skille, Sissel Bjorstad
Nidaroygt. 4
7030 Trondheim, Norway
011-47-7352-9988
sbskille@broadpark.no

Stoehr, Beverly
(see Paradise Galleries)

Tepper, Gloria
10 Plaza St.
Brooklyn, NY 11238
(718) 399-2330

excelxia@yahoo.com

Thompson, Judi L.
PO Box 292
Danville, WA 99121
(205) 442-2857

Tonner, Robert
Tonner Doll Company
459 Hurley Ave.
Hurley, NY 12443
(800) 324-0486
www.tonnerdoll.com

Tucker, Sandi
1245 Carrie Lynn Dr.
Manning, SC 29102
(803) 473-5344
cherished-cherubs@sc.rr.com

Turner, Virginia Ehrlich
Turner Dolls, Inc.
PO Box 36
Heltonville, IN 47436
(800) 887-6372
vturner@kiva.net

Varner, Lori
RR 2, Box 1768
McAlisterville, PA 17049
(717) 463-3632
loartdolls@tricountryi.net

Vogue Doll
Company, The
PO Box 756
Oakdale, CA 95361
(209) 848-0300
Fax: (209) 848-4423
www.voguedolls.com

Webster, Rita
Rita's Art
1109 Crowfoot Ln.
Silver Spring, MD 20904
(202) 418-1993
rdorsey731@comcast.net

Wolf, Peter
Leistenst. No. 1
97082 Worzburg
Germany
011-49-931-83134

Xenis Collection Ltd.
26660 60th Ave.
Aldergrove, B.C.
Canada V4W 1V7
(604) 856-9613
Fax: (604) 856-9623
www.xenis.com

About the Author

JOAN MUYSKENS PURSLEY, a graduate of the University of Iowa's School of Journalism, has spent more than 25 years as a magazine editor and writer. In addition to serving as editorial director of *Dolls* magazine, in which capacity she wrote numerous articles about contemporary doll artists, she has worked for The Iowa State Department of History and Archives, Times Mirror Magazines, Family Media, VNU, Scott Publications and Collector Communications Corporation, where she was the editorial director and associate publisher of the company's three magazines. She has served as editor of *The Annals of Iowa*; *Miniature Collector*; *Dollmaking—Projects and Plans*; *Dolls*; *Figurines and Collectibles*; *Collector Editions* and *Giftware Business*. She is currently editorial director of Art Education for the Blind.

Ms. Pursley is the author of *Wildlife Art: 60 Contemporary Masters & Their Work*, *The World's Most Beautiful Dolls, Volume II*, and co-author, with Karen Bischoff, of volume one of *The World's Most Beautiful Dolls*.